DEMOCRACY AND COMPLEXITY:

who governs the governors?

The Insight Series:

Studies in Contemporary Issues

from The Glencoe Press

Series Editors: Fred Krinsky and Joseph Boskin

DEMOCRACY AND COMPLEXITY: who governs the governors?

Fred Krinsky

Professor
Department of Political Science
University of Southern California

THE GLENCOE PRESS
A Division of The Macmillan Company
Beverly Hills, California

JC
330
.K7

First printing, 1968.

Library of Congress catalog card number: 68-22214.

The Glencoe Press.
A Division of The Macmillan Company.
Collier-Macmillan Canada, Ltd., Toronto, Ontario.
Printed in the United States of America.

Preface

There has long been a need to reconsider the realities of American policy-making in terms of democratic ideals. Every citizen, at one time or another, has wondered what difference his voice makes in the policies and laws of this country. An ever greater number of citizens and scholars is questioning the validity of our notion of political values. The fact is that many people, whether or not they approve of the government's policies, feel that they have no real say in running their country.

This book is designed to provide some very rich analyses of the question: Who really governs whom? In Chapter One an article by Edward Shils discusses the ways in which social organization in modern affluent states differs from the patterns of the past. The next two chapters present selections that describe the operation of two different kinds of modern power-groups: informal, *influential* elites; and formalized, *bureaucratic* elites. In Chapter Four, a skillful essay by Richard Goodwin summarizes the problems suggested in earlier pieces and suggests several ways of reuniting the governors with the governed.

The author wishes to express his gratitude to Michael E. Brown, of California State College at Fullerton, for his aid in preparing this volume.

F.K.

Los Angeles, California
November, 1967

(NOTE. — Throughout this book, the author-editor's footnotes are marked by symbols — *, † — and the original quoted notes by numerals.)

Contents

DEMOCRACY AND COMPLEXITY:

who governs the governors?

Chapter One

Introduction

...Never in recent times have the politicians of every party commanded so little credence from the public.

—REGINALD MAULDING, *Deputy Leader*
British Conservative Party

The candor of Reginald Maulding's statement is typically British, but the object of his concern is a public attitude all too common in the United States. It is becoming apparent that public interest and involvement in the governing process have lagged considerably behind the myth of their importance in a democracy. Democratic theory has long stressed the idea that the vitality and longevity of democracy depends almost entirely upon citizens' interest and participation in public affairs; it has also implied that a rational appraisal of public issues and a moderate, orderly exertion of demands upon the political system is necessary as well.

Yet, political behavior in contemporary America belies the theory. Public response to politics alternates between apathy and highly emotional engagement. Demands for change are being more aggressively registered through non-traditional, extra-political pressures and mass demonstrations of protest. The government, which has historically been a mediating agent between private interests and the common need, has become a powerful, self-interested element in recent decades. In fact, one is almost tempted to say that battle lines on major issues are often drawn between *the people* on the one side and *the government* on the other. It is a peculiar and disturbing situation, indeed, when large groups of citizens of a nation based on a precept of "government of the people, by the people, and for the people" begin to view the state with apathy, disdain, and even hostility.

Though the causes for this general public attitude are many and complex, and thus difficult to discern, a glance at some of the radical changes in American society over the past thirty years gives us a clue. The stabilizing of economic cycles, the insistent rise in general affluence, urbanization, and increasing technological complexity have contributed substantially to a civilization of prosperity without historical precedent. And, although many would like to ignore the fact, advances in most areas of American life have been closely related to massive intervention, regulation, and financial involvement by the central government.

The consequent rise of the "service state" has disturbed many for various reasons. The most common complaint concerns an increasing bureaucracy. For every public service there must be an administrative agency, whether on the local, state, or national level of government; and for every agency there must be tax support. As the services increase in scope and number, the agencies multiply in type and size, concurrently becoming more centralized, impersonal, and remote from those whom they are designed to serve. Although this pattern of bureaucratization is lamentable, it is not unique to government. Bigness is common to both the private and public sectors of society, and in fact the complexity and confusion of modern living are directly reflected within government itself. The shame is that the average citizen, coping with his own personal existence, has neither the time nor energy to become knowledgeable about the intricacies of the decision-making processes. His election-time involvement consists largely in choosing between competing political images and styles rather than in registering his judgment on issues and programs.

We say that modern confusion goes deeper into the social structure than even political manifestations can indicate. How has this disintegration of the old norms, the traditions which have related man to man and man to society, come about?

It is the changing nature of society which concerns Edward Shils in the introductory article. In his discussion of civilization in modern states, Shils argues that "the center of society ... has extended its boundaries"; this has, in effect, brought the individual into closer participation in government and greater obedience to political authority. Shils labels this more politicized modern society as a "mass society," and is particularly heartened by the freedom and opportunity it proffers to the average man for the creation of his own authentic identity and mode of life.

The reader should realize, however, that Shils' celebration of the "mass man" is not universally shared. Other writers (for example, Hannah Arendt, Erich Fromm, and William Kornhauser) have assessed twentieth-century societal change in much the same manner as Shils, but come to some fearful conclusions. They perceive an inability of the individual to cope emotionally with the ambiguities and complexities of modern life and argue that a man cannot help but look to a leader or a set of simple explanations (ideology) to make sense of the confusion he feels. These writers imply that given a choice, the mass would opt for authority and state guidance rather than celebrate its own freedom to make choices. Erich Fromm has summed it up by suggesting that while men have freedom from traditional modes and mores, they are confronted by the new problem of what to do with their freedom.

While Shils' hypotheses as to the possibilities of a "new man" are fascinating and provocative, we are most concerned here with his elucidation of society's changing nature. His theory of mass society serves as a general orientation to more specific problems regarding the locations and structures of power in modern America.

The Theory of Mass Society*

Edward Shils

Prefatory Remarks

A specter is haunting sociologists. It is the specter of "mass society." This phantasm is not of the sociologist's own making. The conception of mass society that had its origin in the Roman historians' idea of the tumultuous populace and its greatest literary expression in *Coriolanus* is largely a product of the nineteenth century. In this epoch, it is a product of the reaction against the French revolutions which run from 1789, through 1830 and 1848, to 1871. Jacob Burckhardt and Friedrich Nietzsche, fearful of the inflammability of the mob in the presence of a heated demagogue—that demagogue was Louis Napoleon—came to envisage modern society, particularly modern democratic society, as tending toward

---

*Reprinted with permission of The Macmillan Company from *America as a Mass Society*, Philip Olson, ed. Copyright © The Free Press of Glencoe, a Division of The Macmillan Company, 1963. This article appeared originally in *Diogenes*, No. 39 (Fall, 1962).

an inert and formless mass, lying in brutish torpor most of the time and occasionally aroused to prebliscitary acclamation by a "great simplifier." De Tocqueville's critique of the absolutist *ancien régime*, through its image of a society which has lost its framework of feudal liberty through the destruction of the autonomous corporations and estates on which it rested, is a cornerstone of that construction. The arid zone between the absolute prince and the mass of the population was field for passion and manipulation.

This notion of the mob received a certain amount of subsequent embroidery through the work of LeBon and Sighele. A deeper supplementation, which was not drawn at the time, lay in the work of the German sociologists. They distinguished between *Gemeinschaft* and *Gesellschaft*;* the latter, characterized by the evaporation of moral bonds, the shrivelling of kinship and traditional institutions and beliefs, and the isolation of the individual from his fellows, was alleged to correspond to modern Western society.

The synthesis of these elements took place in the quasi-Marxist assessments of the regime of National Socialist Germany. The disintegrative influence of capitalism and urban life had left man alone and helpless. To protect himself, he fled into the arms of the all-absorbing totalitarian party. Thus the coup d'état of Louis Napoleon of December, 1851, and the *Machtergreifung*† of March, 1933, became the prototypical events of modern society, and the society of the Weimar Republic was declared to be the characteristic pattern of modern society in preparation for its natural culmination.

This is the intellectual background from which the conception of mass society has grown. It has gained new strength from the developments in the technology of communication, which were called "mass communications" before their association with mass society occurred. Yet the accident of similar designation has facilitated the fusion of the criticism of the intellectual and cultural content of press, wireless, and television with the apprehension about the standardless and defenseless masses.

The result is the following image of "mass society": a territorially extensive society, with a large population, highly urbanized and industrialized. Power is concentrated in this society, and much of the power takes the form of manipulation of the mass through the

---

*Both of these German nouns can be translated as "association" or "partnership"; but the former has the connotation of mutuality, community, which *Gesellschaft* lacks.

†Literally, "power-grab."

media of mass communication. Civic spirit is poor, local loyalties are few, primordial solidarity is virtually non-existent. There is no individuality, only a restless and frustrated egoism. It is like the state of nature described by Thomas Hobbes, except that public disorder is restrained through the manipulation of the elite and the apathetic idiocy of the mass. The latter is broken only when, in a state of crisis, the masses rally around some demagogue.

I think that this is an untruthful picture of Western society of recent decades. It is a gross distortion of certain features of the large-scale liberal–democratic societies of the West. It is taken from a standpoint which postulates, as the right ordering of life, an entirely consensual, perfectly integrated, small-scale society, permeated by a set of common theological beliefs which give meaning to every aspect of life. Empirically, this view is blind to the whole range of phenomena indicated in this paper; theoretically, it fails to see that no society could go on reproducing itself and maintaining even a coerced order if it corresponded to the description given by the critics of mass society. Yet the conception of mass society has the merit of having responded, however erroneously, to a characteristic feature of this recent phase of modern society; namely, the entry of the mass of the population into greater proximity to the center of society. Although I think that most of the analysis contained in the prevailing conception of this form of twentieth-century Western society is incorrect, it has the virtue of having perceived a certain historical uniqueness and of having given it a name.

The name does not appeal to me. I use it with much misgiving because it has cognitive and ethical overtones which are repugnant to me. Yet, since it has the merit of having focussed attention on a historically and sociologically very significant phase of modern society, and since it is the resultant analysis which I wish to correct, I shall go on using the term, while trying not to be a captive of the problems and categories which it carries with it in its overtones. Furthermore, there is no other term which has a comparable evocative power.

I

The term *mass society* points generally and unsteadily at something genuinely novel in the history of human society. It refers to a new order of society which acquired visibility between the two World Wars, and actually came noisily and ponderously into our presence after the end of the Second. In the United States above all, but also in Great Britain, France, Germany, Northern Italy, the Low and Northern European Countries, Australia, and Japan, this new society has become tangibly established. Less evenly and more partially, some of its features have begun to appear in Eastern and Central Europe and they have here and there begun to show incipient and premonitory signs of existence in Asian and African countries.

The novelty of the mass society lies in the relationship of the mass of the population to the center of the society. The relationship is a closer integration into the central institutional and value systems of the society.

An aggregate of individual human beings living over a territory constitutes a society by virtue of their integration into a system in which the parts are interdependent. The types of societies with which we are concerned here are those in which the integration occurs, not through kinship, but through the exercise and acceptance of authority in the major subsystems of the society, in the polity, the economy, and the status and cultural orders, i.e., in educational and religious institutions and their associated norms and beliefs. Integration occurs in two directions—vertically and horizontally. A society is vertically integrated in a hierarchy of power and authority and a status order; it is horizontally integrated by the unity of the elites of the various sectors of life or subsystems of the society.

The absolutist societies of the European *ancien régime*, and indeed the great monarchies of the Orient and of Western antiquity, were characterized from time to time by a fairly high degree of horizontal integration of the elites at each level of the society; although as one descended in the hierarchy, the territorial radius within which the elites were horizontally integrated diminished. There was a close affinity and cooperation between the governmental, political, religious, military, and intellectual elites, although these were often severe struggles within the political elite which spread to the elites of other spheres. Vertically, however, these societies were very seldom very highly integrated. Villages, estates, regions lived their own lives, connected with the center through the payment of taxes, the provision of obligatory labor services, the performance of religious rites in which the central authority had an acknowledged place and the occasional recourse to a more or less unitary judiciary. These connections were, on the whole, highly intermittent. The major continuous integration from the center was through the church, where, as in Europe, such existed, or through common religious beliefs where there was no formal ecclesiastical body, countrywide in the comprehensiveness of its coverage. The central institutions of government, education, and religion did not reach very far into the life of the mass. The cultural, economic, and administrative autonomy of territorially restricted areas was great, and the center intruded into local life only occasionally. The symbols of the center to which there was a widespread, highly continuous, and common attachment were practically nonexistent. The very meagre coverage of the educational system meant that the culture possessed by the educated classes was scarcely shared at all by the vast majority of the population; and, correspondingly, the conception of the world, and the standards of judgment of the various strata of society, must have had little in common. To a limited extent, this feebleness of the vertical integration from the center was probably offset by the closer contacts between the "big house" and the tenants and laborers on the large estates. Even within this short local radius, however, the amount of vertical integration, although fairly strong as regards authority, must have been slight as regards values, because of the very steep hierarchy of status and the profound differences in culture among the various strata.

At the lower levels, the regimes of the great states were hardly integrated at all horizontally. Villages and estates, over the country as a whole, were scarcely in contact with each other either directly through exchange or sympathy or even through their links with the center.

Indeed, it might be said that, except at the level of the highest political, ecclesiastical, administrative, military, and cultural elites, there really was scarcely a society covering a large territory. The mass was a part of this society largely in the ecological sense; it was only faintly part of its moral order, or even, for that matter, of its system of authority except on narrow occasions.

When we turn our attention to advanced modern societies, the situation is quite otherwise. Government is more continuously and effectively in contact with much of the population through the variety and comprehensiveness of its legislation, through the continuity and intensity of administration, through nearly universal public education until well into adolescence. The capital of a country and its major urban centers are no longer centers only to the notabilities of the society, but for the ordinary people as well. The economy of a mass society is much more integrated both horizontally and vertically than has ever been the case in past epochs of history and outside the advanced industrial societies. Whether by a nation-wide market economy, dominated by large nationwide corporations and by central governmental regulation, or by a socialistically planned economy, scarcely any part of the economic order of the society lives in isolation from its rulers or competitors.

The higher level of educational attainment, the higher degree of literacy, and the greater availability of cultural products like books, periodicals, gramophone records, television, and wireless programs spread the culture which was once confined to a narrow circle at the center over a far greater radius. These, and the much greater "politicization" of the population, bring about a historically unique measure of community of culture.

The intensity of vertical integration differs among societies. Federations are less intensely integrated vertically than unitary regimes; regimes with strong local government are less integrated vertically than regimes like France, where local government is largely in the hands of a centrally appointed official; regimes which allow private and parochial schools are less integrated than those which require that everyone receive his education at a state educational institution. The fundamental distinction among societies with a fairly high degree of integration is that between pluralistic and totalitarian regimes. The latter are much more completely integrated vertically.

Their intense vertical integration is reinforced, furthermore, by their almost equally intense horizontal integration. Their horizontal integration is expressed in the unitary structure of their elites. Their elites are, in their functions, differentiated. Only a very small and very simple society could have an elite in which the same persons performed practically all elite tasks. Differentiation of roles and specialization to the roles of the persons who fill them are an unavoidable and monumental fact of any advanced civilization, however much overlap there is among roles and however much passage there might be among them.

II

The mass society is a new phenomenon, but the elements from which it has arisen are not new. The *polis** was its seed; it was nurtured and developed in the Roman idea of a common citizenship

---

*The *polis* was the main political unit of ancient Greece, the city-state.

extending over a vast territory. The growth of the sense of nationality, from an occasional expression prior to the French Revolution to an expanding reality in the social life of the nineteenth century and the early twentieth century, was the course taken by this deepening sense of affinity among the members of diverse strata and regions of modern countries. When the proponents and agents of the modern idea of the nation put forward the view that life on a contiguous, continuous, and common territory, beyond the boundaries of kinship, caste, and religious belief, united the human beings living within that territory into a single collectivity and made language the evidence of that membership, they committed themselves, not often wittingly, to the mass society. The primordial root of territorial location persists—like other primordial things, it can only become attenuated, but never disappear. Language, and all that is contained in language and transmitted by it, becomes the link through which the members of the mass society are bound to each other and to the center. The sharing of a language is the sharing of the essential quality which confers membership in society.

The sense of the primordial and attachment to it has been transformed and dispersed in mass society. Common existence on a contiguous territory has passed ahead of biological kinship, which obviously has insuperable limitations as a criterion with respect to which union over a large territory is possible. At the most, it is capable of extension into ethnicity and in this transmutation, it has great vitality. The criterion of territoriality is capable of greater extension. It is the rise to prominence of the criterion of territoriality which is one of the main features of the modern sense of nationality, which is, in its turn, a precondition for the emergence of mass society. The fact that a man lives in one's own territory, however extensive, now confers on him rights to one's consideration which earlier societies did not know on this scale. The vital thing is that the territory which possesses this capacity to establish communion has become so greatly extended.

This shift in the balance of weight within the category of primordiality has been part of a wider sublimation of the sacred from the primordial to the dispositional. In early modern times, it was a disposition of belief—even of a specific theological belief—which those most involved in authority thought was necessary for the formation of union over a bounded territory. The dominion of this category of assessment of one's fellow man has been lightened to the advantage of a more general inclination to view another human being in accordance with a conception of him as a bearer of less specific dispositions—either entirely personal or more or less civil. The civil disposition is nothing more than the acknowledgment of the legitimacy of the authority—definitely located in persons or offices, or diffuse in the form of the legitimacy of the social order—which prevails over a territory.

This change has made possible a consensus, fundamental and broad, which includes, as fellow men, all those living on a bounded territory acknowledging by their presence the legitimacy of the order and the authorities who prevail there. The inclusion of the entire population in the society or a pronounced tendency towards that inclusion is what makes the mass society.

III

When we say that this new order of mass society is a consensual society, this does not mean, however, that it is completely consensual, a fabric of seamless harmony. The competition and conflict of corporate bodies resting on diverse class, ethnic, professional, and regional identifications and attachments are vigorous and outspoken in this new order of society. So are the unorganized antagonisms of individuals and families of these diverse class, ethnic, professional, and regional sectors. Inequalities exist in mass society and they call forth at least as much resentment, if not more, as they ever did. Indeed, there is perhaps more awareness of the diversity of situation and the conflict of sectional aspirations in this society than in most societies of the past.

What is specific to this modern mass society, with all its conflicts, is the establishment of consensually legitimate institutions within which much of this conflict takes place and which impose limits on this conflict. Parliaments, the system of representation of interests through pressure groups, systems of negotiation between employers and employees, are the novel ways of permitting and confining the conflict of interests and ideals characteristic of modern mass societies. These institutions, the very constitution of the mass society, can exist because a widespread consensus, particularly a consensus of the most active members of the society, legitimates them, and, more fundamentally, because a more general and more amorphous consensus of the less active imposes restraint on the more active when they might otherwise infringe on the constitution. This consensus grows in part from an attachment to the center, to the central institutional system and value order of the society. It is also a product of a newly emergent—at least on such a vast scale —feeling of unity with one's fellow men, particularly within the territorial boundaries of the modern societies.

Hence, despite all internal conflicts bridging and confining them, there are, within the mass society, more of a sense of attachment to the society as a whole, more sense of affinity with one's fellows, more openness to understanding, and more reaching out of understanding among men than in any earlier society of our Western history or in any of the great Oriental societies of the past. The mass society is not the most peaceful or "orderly" society that has ever existed; but it is the most consensual.

The maintenance of public peace through apathy and coercion in a structure of extremely discontinuous interaction is a rather different thing from its maintenance through consensus in a structure of a more continuous interaction between center and periphery and among various peripheral sectors. The greater activity of the periphery of the society, both in conflict and in consensus—especially in the latter—is what makes this a mass society. The historical uniqueness of the modern society, notably in its latter-day phases, is the incorporation of the mass into the moral order of its society. The mass of the population is no longer merely an object which the elite takes into account as a reservoir of military and labor power or as a possible or actual source of public disorder. Nor does it any longer consist of a set of relatively discrete local societies occasionally in contact with the center under the impulsion of coercion and interest.

The center of society—the central institutions governed by the elites and the central value systems which guide and legitimate these institutions—has extended its boundaries. A center still exists and must always exist; and this entails an inevitable unevenness of the participation in the consensus formed around the center. It is, however, now an unevenness which slopes less steeply, so that most of the population—the "mass"—stand in a closer moral affinity and in a more frequent, even though mediated, interaction with the center than has been the case in either pre-modern societies or the earlier phases of modern society. The greater proximity to the center of society consists of a greater attachment to that center— to the institutions which constitute it and the values which are embodied in it. There is, accordingly, a greater feeling within the mass of being continuous with it, of being part of it, and of its being a part of the same substance of which one is oneself formed.

This consensus has not, however, been unilaterally formed, and it is not sustained merely by the affirmation at the periphery of what emanates from the center, in which the mass has come to share the standards and beliefs of the elites. It consists also in the greater attachment of the center to the peripheral sectors of the society. The elites have changed as well as the masses. One feature of the mass society is that, at least to some extent and in various ways, the elites have come to share many of the objects of attention and fundamental standards which originate, or at least have their main support, in the mass. Of course, elite and mass are not identical in their outlooks or tastes, but the mass means more to elites now than it did in other great societies. It has come to life in the minds of its rulers more vividly than ever before. This change has been brought about in part by the increased political, and then the increased purchasing power of the mass; but, ultimately and profoundly, from the change in moral attitudes which has underlain the enhancement of the dignity of ordinary people. The enhanced dignity of the mass, the belief that, in one way or another, *vox populi, vox dei,* is the source of the mass society. Both elites and the masses have received this into their judgment of themselves and the world; and, although they believe in much else, and believe in this quite unequally, the maxim which locates the sacred in the mass of the population is the shaping force of the most recent development in society.

The sacredness of authority diminished with the dispersal of the sacred into the mass of the population. It is still an object of awe. Charisma is still attributed to it. The awe-inspiring, charismatic quality of authority can never be completely eradicated. Even in mass society, the charisma of the elite is alive, and not solely as a survival from an earlier epoch. It is simply given in the nature of power. The unique feature of the mass society is, however, the dispersion of charismatic quality more widely throughout the society, so that everyone who is a member of the society, because he is a member, comes to possess some of it.

This diminution in the status of authority is part of the same process which loosens the hold of traditional beliefs, especially those promulgated and espoused by hierarchical institutions. A society entirely without tradition is inconceivable. Traditions continue to exert their influence; but they are less overtly acknowledged, somewhat more ambiguous, and more open to divergent interpretations.

The diminished weight of primordiality, the greater concentration on the disposition of those residing at the moment on the bounded territory means that the mass society is the society of the living, contemporaneous mass. It is almost as if society possessed a quantum of charisma, which, if it be attributed to the living, leaves little over for attribution to the ancestors. Since, however, no society can ever cut itself off from its past as a source of its own legitimacy, any more than its sensitivity to the primordial can ever evaporate completely, the traditional inheritance is adapted to the necessities of mass society by the diverse interpretations of rights which correspond to the vital heterogeneity of interests within the mass society itself.

The attenuation of traditional belief and of attachment to the past is accentuated by the less authoritative relationship of adults to children—which in itself is an outcome of the same moral shift which has enabled modern society to become a mass society. The dispersal of the charisma which confers dignity may be observed in the attitudes toward the working classes, women, youth, and ethnic groups that have hitherto been in a disadvantageous position. It is noticeable within families in the rights of children, and within corporate bodies like factories, universities, and churches in the rights of subordinates.

IV

This dispersion of charisma from the center outward has manifested itself in a greater stress on individual dignity and individual rights in all generations, in all strata, in both sexes, and in the whole variety of ethnic groups and peoples. This extension does not always reach equally into all spheres of life; and it does not equally embrace all sectors of the population. Inequalities remain, partly from tradition, partly from functional necessity, and partly from the fact that the movement toward equality is not the only fundamental impulse that moves men and women. Sadism, pride, interest, awe before the creative, still persist and limit the spread of equality.

Nonetheless, this consensus, which leans toward the interpretation of every living human being as a participant in the uniting essence which defines the society has produced a wide distribution of civility. Civility is the virtue of the citizen, not the virtue of the hero or of the private man. It is the acceptance of the tasks of the management of public affairs in collaboration with others and with a regard to the interests, individual, sectional, and collective, of the entire society. The sense of responsibility for and to the whole, and a general acceptance of the rules which are valid within it, are integral to civility. Civil politics are the politics of effective compromise within an institutional system accepted as of inherent legitimacy. The idea of civility is not a modern creation; but it is in the mass society that it has found a more widely diffused, if still a deeply imperfect, realization. The very idea of a citizenry practically coterminous with the adult population living within far-flung territorial boundaries is a product of this extension of the "center," i.e., of the belief that charisma belongs in the mass as well as in the elite.

The moral equalitarianism which is such a unique trait of the West, in real practice and not just as the dream of philosophers, is another manifestation of this expansion of the "center."[1] The moral equality which has a tangible reality in mass societies is the equality which is a function of the sharing in membership in a community, by the sharing of the language in which the essence of the society is expressed. Those who share in this membership, as it is evinced by their share in the language, come to be regarded as sharing in the charismatic essence of the society and therewith may legitimately claim an irreducible dignity.

V

The mass society lifted the lid on impulse, hitherto held down by the hierarchy of authority, tradition, and ancestry. The relocation of the charisma of the social order into one's ordinary, individual fellow man marches hand in hand with a redirection of sensitivity to disposition, to qualities lying within the individual. The civil disposition is only one such disposition. There is also the personal disposition which has been increasingly discovered in mass society. It is discovered in oneself and in others.

The personal dispositions, those qualities of rationality and impulsiveness, amiability and surliness, kindliness and harshness, lovingness and hatefulness, are the constitution of the individual. Felt by himself, acknowledged by himself, coped with by himself,

---

[1] In a society touched by moral equalitarianism, the possibility of a populistic inequalitarianism in which some become "more equal than others" is by no means remote. In American society and, possibly, in Australia, which have gone farther in this direction than any other countries, and where populism is not merely a doctrine of the intellectuals but a belief and practice of the populace and its politicians, there is always some danger that a strong gust of populistic sentiment can distract the civil order. Such was the situation during the years from 1947 to 1954, when the late Senator McCarthy stirred and was carried by the whirlpool of an extreme populism. But it never spread into the entire society; and, in the end, it broke on the rocks of Republican respectability. It remains a latent possibility, inherent in the ethos of mass society.

they are formed into his individuality. The perception and appreciation of individuality in others moves in unison with its development in the self.

Personal individuality and the sacredness of the individual in the civil order are not identical. Indeed, they are almost polar opposites; the latter is in a certain sense a denial of the former. It transcends personal individuality and suspends it. Nonetheless they both have grown from the lightening of pressure of the primordial and from the loosening of the rigor of a sacred order based on common belief, on a shared communion with divinity.

Individuality, personal relationships, and love have not been discovered by mass society. They have been known in practically all cultures. It is, however, only in mass society that they have come to be regarded as part of the right order of life, and have come to be striven for and occasionally, however unstably, attained.

The mass society has gone further in the creation of a common culture than any previous society. Regional cultural variations have diminished as well as those of class and profession and even those of generation. Yet this more widely extended uniformity, which for sheer repressive force might be no smaller or greater than the repression of the more local sectional cultures of the past, has been dialectically connected with the emergence of a greater individuality. The contemporaneity of the value-accent of mass society, the heavier stress on present enjoyment rather than on the obligation of respect towards tradition, involves necessarily an opening to experience. The diminished respect for the sacredness of authority has been accompanied by the shift of the center of gravity into the individual. Of course, as the critics of mass society often point out, this can result in a dull acceptance of what is readily available in the most visible models in the culture, and in fact it frequently does so, with the result that individuality in many instances is no better situated in mass society than it was in more hierarchical and traditional societies. Nonetheless, there has been a great change, not too different from that which Burckhardt perceived in the Renaissance. The individual organism has become a seeker after experience, a repository of experience, an imaginative elaborator of experience. To a greater extent than in the past, the experience of the ordinary person, at least in youth, is admitted to consciousness and comes to form part of the core of the individual's outlook. There has come about a greater openness to experience, an efflorescence of sensation and sensibility. There has been a transcendence of the primordially and authoritatively given, a movement outward towards experience, not only towards organic sensation, but towards the experience of other minds and personalities. It gives rise to and lives in *personal* attachment, it grows from the expansion of the emphatic capacities of the human being.

In a crude, often grotesque way, the mass society has seen the growth, over wide areas of society, of an appreciation of the value of the experience of personal relationships, of the intrinsic value of a personal attachment, nowhere more than in the vicissitudes of love and marriage in modern society, with all its conflict and disso- lution. Perhaps too much is demanded of the frail and unstable capacities of the organism for personal attachment, but the sensi- tivity and the striving are there. The talk about "human relations" in private and public administration might be largely cant and un- thinking cliché, but not entirely. This is the age in which man has begun to live, to breathe with less congestion and to open his pores. The pleasures of eye and ear and taste and touch and conviviality have become values in larger sections of the population.

People make many choices in many spheres of life and do not have choices made for them simply by tradition, authority, and scarcity. They enjoy some degree of freedom of choice, and they exercise that freedom in more spheres than in societies which are not mass societies. The choices are often unwise, and manifest an unrefined taste. They are often ill considered. But they are choices and not the dumb acceptance of what is given.

Prior to the emergence of modern mass society, the mass of the population lived in a primordial, traditional, hierarchical condition. All of these three properties of a society hamper the formation of individuality and restrict its movement once it is generated. The twin processes of civilization and industrialization have reduced some of these hindrances, and set loose the cognitive, appreciative, and moral potential of the mass of the population.

I would not wish to have the foregoing observations interpreted to imply that the individuality which has flowered in mass society has been an unqualified moral and aesthetic success or that it is universally attained within the boundaries of mass society, or that there are not persons to whom it is not a value, nor am I unaware that in Germany the elite of the society went to the opposite extreme and that many of its members enthusiastically and brutally denied the value of individual human existence. A significant proportion of the population in every society lives in a nearly vegetative routine, withdrawn and unresponsive except for occasional patches of harsh aggressive expansiveness. In the mass society of the present century, the proportion seems smaller, the period of sensitivity in the individual's course of life longer.

Personal relations, friendship and love, are beset by vicissitudes and frequently culminate in painful disruption; sensibility and curiosity are often perverse and injurious. Privacy is frequently affronted and transgressed and frequently indiscriminately renounced. In certain sections of the population, the discovery of the possibility and pleasures of sensation have been carried to the far reaches of a negative withdrawal from society and of an often active rejection. In others, it releases an egoistic hedonism, an individual expansiveness which leaves nothing available to the civil sphere and the consensus which it requires.

Some of these are as much the products of man's nature amidst the possibilities of mass society as are the heightened individuality, curiosity, and sensibility, the enhanced capacity for experience, conviviality, and affection, which are its novel contributions. They are the price which is paid for entering into the opening of human potentialities on a massive scale.

VI

The mass society is a welfare society. As a function of a greater attachment to the whole society and the strengthening of the sense of affinity which cuts across class, ethnic, and kinship boundaries, there has grown the concern for the well being of others. Christianity as a body of specific beliefs might have faded from men's minds — although probably not as much as the *laudator temporis acta** insists — but the sentiment embodied in the idea of Christian charity and Christian love has expanded and spread. These are now a part of the constitution of mass society — in the allegedly "secular state." Material help and emotional sympathy may be claimed without specific payment or counter-performance. Regardless of whether the economic regime is nominally socialistic or capitalistic, and whether the ruling political party regards itself as socialist or bourgeois, it is commonly acknowledged that, at least at the lower levels of the social and economic scale, there need not be any commensurate relationship between specific performance and reward. In the corporate bodies which conduct the main industrial and commercial activities of the mass society, trade union principles and the practices of personnel management have eroded the standard that rewards must be precisely correlated to specific performances in a role. This process, like the other processes which characterize mass society, has its

---

*Freely translated: "the cry of the times."

limitations. It comes into conflict with the exigencies of operation of any large-scale undertaking which require impersonal administration in accordance with reasonably explicit and differentiated rules. The requirement of a modicum of efficiency, and of justice too, requires a measure of specificity in the standards which govern the allocation of opportunity for access to many occupational roles. It requires also a fixation of the rules governing rights and obligations in the society at large and within particular corporate bodies.

VII

Mass society is an industrial society. Without industry, i.e., without the replacement of simple tools by complicated machines, mass society would be intellectually inconceivable and actually impossible. Modern industrial technique through its creation of an elaborate network of transportation and communication has rendered it possible for the various parts of mass society to have a frequency of contact with each other that is unknown to earlier, non-industrial societies. The different social classes and regional sectors of a society can become more aware of each other's modes of life. This heightened mutual awareness, impossible without the modern technology of communication and transportation, has enlarged the internal population which dwells in the minds of men.

Modern industrial technique makes possible and requires the proliferation of the intellectual professions. It has produced the education which, numerous though its deficiences might be, has, through reading and instruction, opened the mind to the varieties of experience of other human beings. It has liberated man from the burden of physically exhausting labour; it has given him a part of each day and week free from the discipline and strain of labour; and it has given him resources through which new experiences of sensation, expansion into conviviality, and interior elaboration have become realities.

Mass society has witnessed a reinterpretation of the value of a human being. Simply by virtue of his quality of membership in the society he acquires a minimal dignity.

The elevation of the *qualities* of humanity and of membership in a wider, territorially circumscribed community to a position in which they markedly determine the status and right of individuals, groups and classes, has led to a diminution of the importance of individual *achievement* as a standard for the direction of one's own actions and as a criterion of status. The increased value of experience, of pleasurable experience, most easily obtainable in mass society through the cultivation of style of life, has had a parallel effect. The quality of life has tended—the nature of man would never allow it wholly to succeed—to replace occupational achievement and proficiency as a source of self-esteem and as a criterion for esteeming others.

This produces a grandiose historical paradox. Mass society, which has been made possible by technological and economic progress, which in turn has been impelled by the desire for achievement for the proficient performance of a role, contributes toward a situation in which occupational role and achievement have become less important in the guidance of action and in the claiming and acknowledgment of status.

A large-scale society requires large-scale bureaucratic administration. Its well-being depends on technological progress. Both of these depend on the wide distribution in the population of individuals capable of acting in the light of impersonal, universalistic standards, capable of performing specific and specialized tasks, capable of discipline. All of these are alien to the characteristic ethos of mass society. The disjunction can only make for an incessant tension of the mass of the population and in many personalities towards the value-orientations required by the type of society to which contemporary men are committed by the circumstances of their birth and their own desires.

VIII

The mass society is a large-scale society. It involves populations running into the millions and hundreds of millions and it covers large territories. It is therefore inevitably a differentiated society, differentiated in function, outlook, and attachments. The complete homogeneity which the critics of mass society perceive is an impossibility. There is, of course, perhaps a greater homogeneity than in the much less loosely integrated societies of the past—this is given in the fact of the great consenuality, the greater sense of unity, the speaking of a common language. There are, however, real although probably undeterminable limits to the homogeneity which any large-scale society can sustain. Similar limits are imposed on the consensuality of the society, even if it had not inherited such a variety of cultural traditions of class-orientations and religious beliefs.

IX

The picture which I have given here will immediately strike any moderately informed person as widely at variance with the image of the mass society which has been set going by the creators and the patrons of that term. They have stressed alienation, belieflessness, atomization, amorality, conformity, rootless homogeneity, moral emptiness, facelessness, egotism, and the utter evaporation of any kind of loyalty (except occasionally the passionately zealous attachment to an ideological movement). They point to the indiscipline of youth and the neglect of the aged; they allege a frivolous hedonism and a joyless vulgarity. There is a little truth in these assertions but not very much. All of the phenomena referred to do exist in modern mass societies, but a great deal more exists. Some of the features to which the critics of mass society point are closely connected with these others which I have emphasized. The alienation so often mentioned is an extreme form of the disenchantment (*Entzauberung*) of authority; the unchecked egotism and frivolous hedonism are associated with the growth of individual sensibility; and the indiscipline of youth is a product of the lightening of the force of the primordial and the diminished pressure of hierarchy. The narrowing of the scope of local autonomy is connected with the formation of a more integral society. The apathy, which so many notice, is brought to the forefront of attention as a result of the greatly extended opportunity for judgment and sharing in the exercise of decision which mass society offers. The vulgarity is one of the manifestations of the expansion of sensibility; it is an unrefined and unappealing expression of sensibility which replaces the long prevailing torpor of much of the race.

The consensuality of mass society, the closer approximation of center and periphery, the greater moral equality of the various strata and sectors, the growth of sensibility and individuality are all, as I have said, imperfect. Their imperfection comes from the inherent impossibility for any large-scale society to attain perfection in those categories, or of any society to attain perfection in any category. The imperfections of mass society are in part a result of the distribution of moral qualities in human beings. In part they come from the nature of mass society as such and its inheritance from the past of mankind.

Mass society has arisen from an inegalitarian, pluralistic society, pluralistic out of the separateness of the classes, the isolation of localities from each other, and, in modern times, the very principle of organization of society. It has arisen against a background of puritanical authority which, whatever its own practices, viewed with disapproval the pleasures of the mass of the population and of all that seemed to distract them from their twin obligations of labour and obedience. The proletariat of these past societies, except for a few skilled occupations with elaborate traditions of their own, were a poor, besotted lot; the peasantry were clods, sometimes woodenly pious, sometimes simply woodenly dull. In so far as they had loyalties, they were strictly local. There is practically no history of civility in the lower classes of pre-modern societies and it appears only fitfully, albeit impressively, among the highest level of the artisan stratum in the nineteenth century.

The emancipation of the hitherto disadvantaged classes from the burdensome moral traditions and the sheer poverty and heavy labour which confined the development of their emotional and moral potentialities let loose, together with the more positive striving for experience and pleasure, a hitherto suppressed anti-authoritarian aggressiveness. The transfer of a certain amount of libido from kinship, class, and ethnic groups to the larger community has not been a readily encompassable task. In many cases, the old loyalties have fallen away and the larger loyalty has not replaced them. It is quite possible that many human beings, lack the capacity to sustain a loyalty to such remote symbols and they are, in consequence, left suspended in apathy and dissatisfaction between narrower loyalties no longer effective—and they probably were never very effective for most—and broader loyalties not yet effective—and perhaps never to become effective for all.

None of these conditions has been very conducive to the realization of a civil, cultivated, consensual, more egalitarian society, quite apart from ineluctable functional constraints.

X

Can it ever be fully realized? Can mass society move forward to the fulfillment of the possibilities which have been opened by technological progress and the moral transmutation arising from the shift in the locus of charisma?

There are very stringent limitations. There are limitations which the trend towards moral equality must encounter because the propensities which impel men to seek and acknowledge a measure of fundamental moral equality are neither deeper nor more enduring than those which demand and produce moral inequality. A large-scale society will necessarily be regionally differentiated and this will entail differences in interests and loyalties. The natural differences in intellectual capacities and in temperament will inevitably make for differences in assimilation of the central value system.

Occupational differences will sustain different streams of cultural tradition, different orientations to the principle of achievement, and different relationships to the authorities at the heart of the central institutional system. And naturally, the differences of age and the culture of the various generations will also be a source of fissure. These differences are all anchored in "objective" differences, inevitably associated with the human lot in general or with the unavoidable conditions of any large-scale industrial society. They are objective differences on which the dispositions toward evaluative discrimination will always seize. Then, too, there is not only the need for communion. There is the need for separation and distance—collective as well as individual—which will create, in any society, lines of fissure in the surface of union and in the sense of moral equality which attends it.

For the same reasons, the full realization of a common culture is an impossibility. The growth of individuality is another obstacle which stands in the way of an all-comprehending growth of a common culture. The growth of individuality too has its limits, imposed in part by the other features of mass society and, in part, by the wide range of dispersion among human beings of the intensity of need for individuality.

Finally, the propensities which have been released and cultivated by the mass society are not harmonious with the relatively remote goals. And it requires, too, a complex division of labor, with many occupational and professional roles, some of which are highly creative and others quite routine, some of which will be highly remunerated and others less so. Equality of status will not grow from these occupational and income differences. Some of these occupations will call for and nurture dispositions which are contrary to the diffusely equalitarian, consensual, hedonistic, affective humanitarian tendencies inherent in mass society. The dispositions to primordial attachment will also persist—kinship and its ethnic sublimation, locality, sexuality might be further transmuted in mass society but they can never be eradicated. They will continue to be at war with the elements which constitute mass society and with those required for a large-scale society. Thus there is likely always to be tension among these diverse sets of elements, which are so dependent on each other. Each will limit the expansion of the others and contend against them and will prevent the society from ever becoming wholly a mass society. But the tension will never be able to prevent these properties of the mass society from finding a grandiose expression.

The potentiality for the mass society has always lain within the human soul. It could only find its opportunity for realization in the peculiar conjuncture of spiritual, political, and technological events which are at the basis of modern society. It comes into realization in an age when the human race is for the first time in its history in considerable prospect of extinction at its own hands, and that comes as the result of skills which were essential to the ideals of the Enlightenment and to the genesis of mass society. Yet, even if the race were to end, the philosophers of the Enlightenment, or their heirs who would be born in a new beginning, would have to admit that their ideals had not been vainly espoused and that the race had not ended before many of their deepest ideals had been attained.

Chapter Two

Locations of Power: Influential Elites

Social scientists have long been aware that elected political decision-makers feel themselves accountable to two major elements in society: (1) the voters whom they officially represent, and (2) the *influential* elites: powerful unofficial interest groups which exert informal influence on the resolution of specific issues. American politicians must tread a precarious path between the public interest and the multiplicity of private interests.

Still another major source of political pressure has developed during the last twenty years. The rise of the welfare state and the expansion of a permanent system of Cold-War military defense have created a third bastion of power: *bureaucratic* elites within the government. Just as private pressure groups attempt to protect their interests in the political process, so also agencies of government desire to defend their programs, functions, and institutional prerogatives against attack and possible mutation at the hands of Congress or the president. Elected representatives, as a result, have recently found themselves confronted with a third and new major force which they must somehow balance against the older ones.

The examination of such bureaucratic elites is the function of Chapter Three. The analyses in the present chapter deal primarily with the nature and operation of the unofficial influential elites, which themselves have become increasingly complex and powerful in contemporary America.

In the first selection, David Riesman, sociologist, lawyer and author of many provocative works other than *The Lonely Crowd,* which is excerpted here, describes these private groups and their changing modes of influencing public policy.

Images of Power*

David Riesman

In the United States the more opulent citizens take great care not to stand aloof from the people; on the contrary, they constantly keep on easy terms with the lower classes; they listen to them, they speak to them every day. They know that the rich in democracies always stand in need of the poor, and that in democratic times you attach a poor man to you more by your manner than by benefits conferred.

—ALEXIS DE TOCQUEVILLE, *Democracy in America*

There has been in the last fifty years a change in the configuration of power in America, in which a single hierarchy with a ruling class at its head has been replaced by a number of *veto groups* among which power is dispersed. This change has many complex roots and complex consequences, including the change in political mood from moralizing to tolerance. A clear-cut power structure helped to create the clarity of goals of the inner-directed; an amorphous power structure helps to create the consumer orientation of the other-directed.†

---

*Chapter X from *The Lonely Crowd* by David Riesman (New Haven, Conn.: Yale University Press, 1961), pp. 206–23. Copyright © 1950, 1953, 1961 by Yale University Press.

†One of Riesman's most noted contributions to social theory has been his distinction between *inner-directed* people, whose desires and opinions come from within themselves; and *other-directed* people, who draw their motivations and ideas largely from the groups they belong to. Riesman here suggests that this contrast is to some extent a distinction beween producers and consumers of ideas.

The Leaders and the Led

There have been two periods in American history in which a sharply defined ruling class emerged. In the late eighteenth and early nineteenth centuries the Federalist leadership—landed-gentry and mercantilist-money leadership—certainly thought of itself as, and was, a ruling group. Long before its leadership was actually dislodged, its power was disputed and, in decisive instances, overruled in the northern and middle states by yeoman farmers and artisans. These latter, having little time or gift for politics, ordinarily left it to their "betters," but they retained a veto on what was done and occasionally, as with Jackson, moved into a more positive command. After the Civil War, however, farmers and artisans lost their capacity to check what was done, and the captains of industry emerged as a ruling class. During their hegemony the images and the actualities of power in America coincided more closely than I think they do today.

Captains of Industry and Captains of Consumption

According to this view of the matter, the election of 1896 appears as an historical watershed: the high point of oligarchic rule. In terms of political style, there were moralizers for Bryan and moralizers for McKinley. And there were groups that, whether or not they saw their interests in moral terms, had a clear picture of themselves and of their interests; they, too, responded to the election in an inner-directed way. Only a few people like Brooks Adams, who supported Bryan out of his hatred for the "goldbugs," were aware of some of the ambiguities in the positions of both candidates.

Certainly, the victorious leaders—McKinley, Hanna, and Morgan in their several bailiwicks—were not aware of ambiguity. The success of their electoral bid is less important to us than the mood of their undertaking, which was one of conscious leadership, directed by conscious class considerations. The self-conscious leadership took support from the close connection, to which I have already called attention, between politics and work. The world of work was the great world; politics was an extension that could either facilitate work or sabotage it. While bankers and Grangers had different notions as to what work politics should do and what leave undone, they agreed as to the primacy of the production side of life.

Of course, the political sphere was not devoid of entertainment for the inner-directed man: with its opportunity for cracker-barrel argument, beer drinking, and shirt-sleeved goodfellowship by torch-light, it had its occasional uses as a "downward" escape from the dignities of work and the propertied existence. But the great differ-ence from today is that the leaders went into politics to do a job—primarily to assure the conquest of American resources—rather than to seek a responsive audience. As Rockefeller sold his oil more by force or cheapness than by brand, so the late nineteenth-century political leader sold his wares (votes or decisions) to the highest bidder. Either cash or morality might bid—but not "good will" as such.

This situation and these inner-directed motivations gave a clarity to the political and social scene in 1896 that it does not appear to have had in De Tocqueville's day and has not had since. The bullet that killed McKinley marked the end of the days of explicit class leadership. Muckraking and savage political cartooning—arts that depend on clarity of line—continued for a time and of course have not quite vanished yet. But as the old-time religion depended on a clear image of heaven and hell and clear judgments of good and evil, so the old-time politics depended on a clear class structure and the clear and easily moralized judgments of good and bad that flow from it. It depended, too, and I cannot emphasize the point too much, on an agreement between leaders and led that the work sphere of life was dominant. And because the goals were clear, the obvious job of the leader was to lead; of the led, to follow. Their political cooperation, like their cooperation in industry and agriculture, was based on mutual interests, whether directly moralized or not, rather than on mutual preferences and likings.

What I have said must be taken as an "ideal-typical" political portrait of the age, useful by way of contrast to our own times. Actually, the changes are, as always, changes in emphasis and de-gree, and the portrait would be seriously overdrawn if the reader should conclude that no emotional moods, no cravings for charisma and glamor, eddied about the relations between leaders and led. These relations were not built entirely out of sober moralizing and well-understood economic interests, but occasionally, as Veblen described matters, the Captain of Industry served to provide the underlying population with personages to admire "to the greater spiritual comfort of all parties concerned."

Ruling-class theories, applied to contemporary America, seem to be spectral survivals of this earlier time. The captain of industry no longer runs business, no longer runs politics, and no longer pro-vides legitimate "spiritual comfort." Here and there, it is true, there are survivals. In the booming Southwest, Texas still produces men like Glenn McCarthy, and California produced an old-style lion of the jungle in A. P. Giannini (who was, significantly enough, from a family which lacked the opportunity to educate him for the newer business motivations). Yet even these types are touched by traits that were not nearly so evident in the earlier captains of industry who fascinated Veblen as Lucifer fascinated Milton. Like Henry Kaiser, they depend much more than did the older magnificoes on public opinion and, as a corollary to public opinion, on the attitude of government. To this end they tend to exploit their personalities, or allow them to be exploited, in a way that makes the elder Rockefeller's Ivy Lee stunt of dime-giving seem as remote as the Fuggers.

Much more than their pre-World War I predecessors, then, these surviving captains stay within the limits as well as the possibilities of the economy of the glad hand. If they enter politics they do so because it is a sport or obligation for the rich ; or simply because they are tied in with government at every step in their ramifying enterprises. These latter-day captains neither see themselves nor are recognized as political leaders who, by their presence and by what they stand for, clarify and thereby moralize politics. The elder Morgan and his friends thought it was up to them to stop Bryan and to stop the depression of 1907. No one has taken their place.

In the focus of public attention the old captains of industry have been replaced by an entirely new type : the Captains of Non-industry, of Consumption and Leisure. Surveys of content in the mass media show a shift in the kinds of information about business and political leaders that audiences ask for.[1] In an earlier day the audience was given a story of the hero's work-minded rise to success. Today, the ladder climbing is taken for granted or is seen in terms of "the breaks," and the hero's tastes in dress, food, women, and recreation are emphasized—these are, as we have seen, the frontiers on which the reader can himself compete, while he cannot imagine himself in the work role of the president of the United States or the head of a big company.

What is more, there is a shift in such biographies from an accent on business leaders to an accent on "leaders" in consumption. Proportionately, actors, artists, entertainers, get more space than they

---

[1] See the excellent article by Leo Lowenthal, "Biographies in Popular Magazines," *Radio Research, 1942–43*, ed. Lazarsfeld and Stanton (New York: Duell, Sloan & Pearce, 1944), p. 507. Dr. Lowenthal links the shift from "heroes of production" to "heroes of consumption" to major social changes in American life.

used to, and the heroes of the office, hustings, and factory get less. These consumers of the surplus product may, in Veblen's terms, provide "spiritual comfort" by their very skill in consumption. The glamor of such heroes of consumption may reside in their incompetence in the skills of businesslike performance and, as we have seen, in some cases their wholly personal "sincerity" may do duty in place of more objective artistic criteria.

But, of course, these captains of consumption are not leaders. They are still only personalities, employed to adorn movements, not to lead them. Yet the actual leaders have much in common with them.

For an illustration we can turn to a recent American leader—undoubtedly a leader—who shared many characteristics of the artist and entertainer: Franklin D. Roosevelt. We are accustomed to thinking of him as a man of great power. Yet his role in leading the country into war was very different from that of McKinley or even of Wilson. Think of McKinley pacing the floor of his study, deciding whether or not to ask for a declaration of war on Spain—when he already knew that Spain would capitulate. McKinley felt it was up to him; so did Wilson. Roosevelt felt he could only maneuver within very narrow limits, limits which came close to leaving the decision to the enemy.

Again, if we compare his activities during the war years with those of Churchill, we can see important differences. Churchill led the British in something like the old-time sense of an explicit relation between the leader and the followers. That he led, moreover, as a moralizing leader and not, despite his great personal charm, as a "personality," appeared in the readiness of the electorate to follow him in war and to dispense with him in peace: they were work minded rather than consumption minded about him. Roosevelt on the other hand remained throughout the war, as before, a powerful though tolerant persuader, even conniver and stimulator, of changes in public opinion that he followed with deep concern at all times. Churchill exploited his indignation, Roosevelt his charm.

The obviously real differences in the military situation of Britain and the United States during this period are not sufficient to explain these differences in the mood and method of leadership. Much more important than the wartime differences between the two countries are the differing shifts in political pattern during the last half century. America in the nineties could be led politically and morally. Since then we have entered a social and political phase in which power is dispersed among veto groups. These groups are too many and diverse to be led by moralizing; what they want is too various to be moralized and too intangible to be bought off for cash alone; and what is called political leadership consists, as we could see in Roosevelt's case, in the tolerant ability to manipulate coalitions.

This means that the men who, at an earlier historical period, were political leaders are now busy with the other-directed occupation of studying the feedback from all the others — their constituencies, their correspondents, and friends and enemies within influential pressure groups. The revolution in communications makes this attention possible in ways that were not available to the equally assiduous client–cultivator of an earlier day, who could buy a few editors if he wanted favorable things said. And those who were once the followers have learned the arts of lobbying and publicity. The roll call of nineteenth- and early twentieth-century leaders contains many men who refused to follow their flock: Gladstone and Cleveland, Robert Peel and John Stuart Mill (as M.P.), Woodrow Wilson and Winston Churchill. Even today the need to impose unpopular courses brings to the fore inner-directed types: Cripps, for instance, in England; Stimson and Robert Patterson in this country. Of course, political figures in all ages have been dependent on their following, and opportunism and manipulation are not a twentieth-century discovery. The inner-directed leader, however, was quite conscious of discrepancies between his views and those of others; if he shifted his course, it was still *his* course. Moreover, since he was ambitious, he might well prefer later fame to momentary warmth of response; in any event he did not need to have everybody love him, but only those who mattered for his fortunes.

In his autobiography, John Stuart Mill tells the following story:

> In the pamphlet, "Thoughts on Parliamentary Reform," I had said, rather bluntly, that the working classes, though differing from those of some other countries, in being ashamed of lying, are yet generally liars. This passage some opponent got printed in a placard which was handed to me at a meeting, chiefly composed of the working classes, and I was asked whether I had written and published it. I at once answered "I did." Scarcely were those two words out of my mouth, when vehement applause resounded through the whole meeting.

It is interesting to compare this incident with the practices of certain American public figures who not only would not think of saying anything that might offend an audience but who frequently depart from a prepared text, carefully designed to please a wide audience, in order to mollify the smaller face-to-face group before whom the speech happens to be delivered.

The old-time captain of industry was also a captain of consumption: what standards were set, were set by him. He was also a captain of politics. The new captain of consumption who has usurped his place in the public eye is limited severely to the sphere of consumption—which itself has of course greatly expanded. Today, the personalities from the leisure world, no matter how much loved, lack the strength and the situation for leadership. If a movie star of today tries to put across a political message, in or out of films, he finds himself vulnerable to all sorts of pressures. The movie producer is no more powerful. The Catholics, the Methodists, the organized morticians, the state department, the southerners, the Jews, the doctors, all put their pressure on the vehicle that is being prepared for mass distribution. Piety or decency protects some minority groups that have no lobbies. The movie maker acts as a broker among these veto groups in a situation much too intricate to encourage his taking a firm, moralizing stance. At best, he or someone in his organization may sneak a moral and political message into the film as Roosevelt or someone in his organization sneaked over an appointment or a new coordinating agency. The message, the appointment, the agency—none of them could get very far in the Alice in Wonderland croquet game of the veto groups.

Who Has the Power?

The Veto Groups

The shifting nature of the lobby provides us with an important clue as to the difference between the present American political scene and that of the age of McKinley. The ruling class of businessmen could relatively easily (though perhaps mistakenly) decide where their interests lay and what editors, lawyers, and legislators might be paid to advance them. The lobby ministered to the clear leadership, privilege, and imperative of the business ruling class.

Today we have substituted for that leadership a series of groups, each of which has struggled for and finally attained a power to stop things conceivably inimical to its interests and, within far narrower limits, to start things. The various business groups, large and small, the movie-censoring groups, the farm groups and the labor and professional groups, the major ethnic groups and major regional groups, have in many instances succeeded in maneuvering themselves into a position in which they are able to neutralize those who might attack them. The very increase in the number of these groups, and in the kinds of interests "practical" and "fictional" they are protecting, marks, therefore, a decisive change from the lobbies of an earlier day. There is change in method, too, in the way the groups are organized, the way they handle each other, and the way they handle the public, that is, the unorganized.

These veto groups are neither leader-groups nor led-groups. The only leaders of notional scope left in the United States today are those who can placate the veto groups. The only followers left in the United States today are those unorganized and sometimes disorganized unfortunates who have not yet invented their group.

Within the veto groups, there is, of course, the same struggle for top places that goes on in other bureaucratic setups. Among the veto groups competition is monopolistic; rules of fairness and fellowship dictate how far one can go. Despite the rules there are, of course, occasional "price wars," like the jurisdictional disputes of labor unions or Jewish defense groups; these are ended by negotiation, the division of territory, and the formation of a roof organization for the previously split constituency. These big monopolies, taken as a single group, are in devastating competition with the not yet grouped, much as the fair-trade economy competes against the free-trade economy. These latter scattered followers find what protection they can in the interstices around the group minded.[2]

Each of the veto groups in this pattern is capable of an aggressive move, but the move is sharply limited in its range by the way in which the various groups have already cut up the sphere of politics and arrayed certain massive expectations behind each cut. Both within the groups and in the situation created by their presence, the political mood tends to become one of other-directed tolerance. The vetoes so bind action that it is hard for the moralizers to conceive of a program that might in any large way alter the relations between political and personal life or between political and economic life. In the amorphous power structure created by the veto groups it is hard to distinguish rulers from the ruled, those to be aided

---

[2]It should be clear that monopolistic competition, both in business and politics, *is* competition. People are very much aware of their rivals, within and without the organization. They know who they are, but by the very nature of monopolistic competition they are seldom able to eliminate them entirely. While we have been talking of fair trade and tolerance, this should not obscure the fact that for the participants the feeling of being in a rivalrous setup is very strong. Indeed, they face the problem of so many other-directed people: how to combine the appearance of friendly, personalized, "sincere" behavior with the ruthless, sometimes almost paranoid, envies of their occupational life.

from those to be opposed, those on your side from those on the other side. This very pattern encourages the inside-dopester who can unravel the personal linkages, and discourages the enthusiast or indignant who wants to install the good or fend off the bad. Probably, most of all it encourages the new-style indifferent who feels and is often told that his and everyone else's affairs are in the hands of the experts and that laymen, though they should "participate," should not really be too inquisitive or aroused.

By their very nature the veto groups exist as defense groups, not as leadership groups. It it is true that they do "have the power," they have it by virtue of a necessary mutual tolerance. More and more they mirror each other in their style of political action, including their interest in public relations and their emphasis on internal harmony of feelings. There is a tendency for organizations as differently oriented as, say, the Young Socialists and the 4-H Club, to adopt similar psychological methods of salesmanship to obtain and solidify their recruits.

This does not mean, however, that the veto groups are formed along the lines of character structure. As in a business corporation there is room for extreme inner-directed and other-directed types, and all mixtures between, so in a veto group there can exist complex symbiotic relationships among people of different political styles. Thus a team of lobbyists may include both moralizers and inside-dopesters, sometimes working in harness, sometimes in conflict; and the constituency of the team may be composed mainly of new-style political indifferents who have enough literacy and organizational experience to throw weight around when called upon. Despite these complications I think it fair to say that the veto groups, even when they are set up to protect a clear-cut moralizing interest, are generally forced to adopt the political manners of the other-directed.

In saying this I am talking about the national scene. The smaller the constituency, of course, the smaller the number of veto groups involved and the greater the chance that some one of them will be dominant. Thus, in local politics there is more indignation and less tolerance, just as even the *Chicago Tribune* is a tolerant paper in comparison with the community throwaways in many Chicago neighborhoods.

The same problem may be considered from another perspective. Various groups have discovered that they can go quite far in the amorphous power situation in America without being stopped. Our society is behaviorally open enough to permit a considerable community of gangsters a comfortable living under a variety of partisan political regimes. In their lack of concern for public relations these men are belated businessmen. So are some labor leaders who have discovered their power to hold up the economy, though in most situations what is surprising is the moderation of labor demands—a moderation based more on psychological restraints than on any power that could effectively be interposed. Likewise, it is sometimes possible for an aggressive group, while not belonging to the entrenched veto-power teams, to push a bill through a legislature. Thus, the original Social Security Act went through Congress, so far as I can discover, because it was pushed by a devoted but tiny cohort; the large veto groups including organized labor were neither very much for it nor very much against it.

For similar reasons those veto groups are in many political situations strongest whose own memberships are composed of veto groups, especially veto groups of one. The best example of this is the individual farmer who, after one of the farm lobbies has made a deal for him, can still hold out for more. The farm lobby's concern for the reaction of other veto groups, such as labor unions, cuts little ice with the individual farmer. This fact may strengthen the lobby in a negotiation : it can use its internal public relations problems as a counter in bargaining, very much as does a diplomat who tells a foreign minister that he must consider how Senator so-and-so will react. For, no matter what the other-directedness of the lobby's leaders, they cannot bind their membership to carry out a public relations approach. Many labor unions have a similar power because they cannot control their memberships who, if not satisfied with a deal made by the union, can walk off or otherwise sabotage a job.

In contrast, those veto groups are often weaker whose other-directed orientation can dominate their memberships. Large corporations are vulnerable to a call from the White House because, save for a residual indignant like Sewell Avery, their officials are themselves other-directed and because, once the word from the chief goes out, the factory superintendents, no matter how boiling mad, have to fall into line with the new policy by the very nature of the centralized organization for which they work : they can sabotage top management on minor matters but not, say, on wage rates or tax accounting. As against this, the American Catholic Church possesses immense veto-group power because it combines a certain amount of centralized command—and a public picture of a still greater amount—with a highly decentralized priesthood (each priest is in a sense his own trade association secretary) and a membership organization of wide-ranging ethnic, social, and political loyalties; this structure permits great flexibility in bargaining.

These qualifications, however, do not change the fact that the veto groups, taken together, constitute a new buffer region between the old, altered, and thinning extremes of those who were once leaders and led. It is both the attenuation of leaders and led, and the other-oriented doings of these buffers, that help to give many moralizers a sense of vacuum in American political life.

The veto groups, by the conditions their presence creates and by the requirements they set for leadership in politics, foster the tolerant mood of other-direction and hasten the retreat of the inner-directed indignants.

Is There a Ruling Class Left?

Nevertheless, people go on acting as if there still were a decisive ruling class in contemporary America. In the postwar years, business-men thought labor leaders and politicians ran the country, while labor and the left thought that "Wall Street" ran it, or the "sixty families." Wall Street, confused perhaps by its dethronement as a telling barom-eter of capital-formation weather, may have thought that the mid-western industrial barons, cushioned on plant expansion money in the form of heavy depreciation reserves and undivided profits, ran the conutry. They might have had some evidence for this in the fact that the New Deal was much tougher with finance capital—e.g., the SEC and the Holding Company Act—than with industrial capital and that when, in the undistributed profits tax, it tried to subject the latter to a stockholder and money-market control, the tax was quickly repealed.

But these barons of Pittsburgh, Weirton, Akron, and Detroit, though certainly a tougher crowd than the Wall Streeters, are, as we saw earlier, coming more and more to think of themselves as trustees for their beneficiaries. And whereas, from the point of view of labor and the left, these men ran the War Production Board in the interest of their respective companies, one could argue just as easily that the WPB experience was one of the congeries of factors that have tamed the barons. It put them in a situation where they had to view their company from the point of view of "the others."

Despite the absence of intensive studies of business power and of what happens in a business negotiation, one can readily get an impres-sionistic sense of the change in business behavior in the last genera-tion. In the pages of *Fortune*, that excellent chronicler of business, one can see that there are few survivals of the kinds of dealings—with other businessmen, with labor, with the government—that were standard operating practice for the pre-World War I tycoons. Moreover, in its twenty-year history, *Fortune* itself has shown, and perhaps it may be considered not too unrepresentative of its audience, a steady decline of interest in business as such and a growing interest in once peripheral matters, such as international relations, social science, and other accoutrements of the modern executive.

But it is of course more difficult to know whether character has changed as well as behavior—whether, as some contend, businessmen simply rule today in a more subtle, more "managerial" way. In "Manager Meets Union" Joseph M. Goldsen and Lillian Low have depicted the psychological dependence of a contemporary sales manager on the approval of the men under him, his willingness to go to great lengths, in terms of concessions, to maintain interpersonal warmth in his relations with them, and his fierce resentment of the union as a barrier to this emotional exchange.[3] As against this, one must set the attitude of some of the auto-supply companies whose leadership still seems much more craft oriented than people oriented and therefore unwilling to make concessions and none too concerned with the emotional atmosphere of negotiations. Likewise, the General Motors–UAW negotiations of 1946, as reported in print, sound more like a cockfight than a Platonic symposium, although in Peter Drucker's *Concept of the Corporation,* a study of General Motors published in the same year, there is much evidence of management eagerness to build a big, happy family.

Power, indeed, is founded, in a large measure, on interpersonal expectations and attitudes. If businessmen feel weak and dependent, they do in actuality become weaker and more dependent, no matter what material resources may be ascribed to them. My impression, based mainly on experiences of my own in business and law practice, is that businessmen from large manufacturing companies, though they often talk big, are easily frightened by the threat of others' hostility; they may pound the table, but they look to others for leadership and do not care to get out of line with their peer-groupers. Possibly, attitudes toward such an irascible businessman as Sewell Avery might mark a good dividing line between the older and the newer attitudes. Those businessmen who admire Avery, though they might not dare to imitate him, are becoming increasingly an elderly minority, while the younger men generally are shocked by Avery's "highhandedness," his rebuff of the glad hand.

---

[3] "Manager Meets Union: a Case Study of Personal Immaturity," *Human Factors in Management,* ed. S. D. Hoslett (Parkville, Missouri: Park College Press, 1946), p. 77.

The desire of businessmen to be well thought of has led to the irony that each time a professor writes a book attacking business, even if almost nobody reads it, he creates jobs in industry for his students in public relations, trade association work, and market research! While the Black Horse Cavalry of an earlier era held up businessmen by threatening to let pass crippling legislation desired by anti-business moralizers, today many honest intellectuals who would not think of taking a bribe hold business or trade association jobs because their clients have been scared, perhaps by these very men, into taking cognizance of some actual or imaginary veto group. Since a large structure is built up to woo the group, no test of power is made to see whether the group has real existence or real strength. Understandably, ideologies about who has power in America are relied upon to support these amiable fictions which serve . . . to provide the modern businessman with an endless shopping list, an endless task of glad-handing. This is a far cry, I suggest, from the opportunistic glad-handing of the wealthy on which De Tocqueville comments at the chapter head; very likely, what was mere practice in his day has become embedded in character in ours.

Businessmen, moreover, are not the only people who fail to exploit the power position they are supposed, in the eyes of many observers, to have. Army officers are also astonishingly timid about exercising their leadership. During the war [World War II] one would have thought that the army would be relatively impervious to criticism. But frequently the generals went to great lengths to refrain from doing something about which a congressman might make an unfriendly speech. They did so even at times when they might have brushed the congressman off like an angry fly. When dealing with businessmen or labor leaders, army officers were, it seemed to me, astonishingly deferential; and this was as true of the West Pointers as of the reservists. Of course, there were exceptions, but in many of the situations where the armed services made concessions to propitiate some veto group, they rationalized the concessions in terms of morale or of postwar public relations or, frequently, simply were not aware of their power.

To be sure, some came to the same result by the route of a democratic tradition of civilian dominance. Very likely, it was a good thing for the country that the services were so self-restrained. I do not here deal with the matter on the merits but use it as an illustration of changing character and changing social structure.

All this may lead to the question: Well, who really runs things? What people fail to see is that, while it may take leadership to start things running, or to stop them, very little leadership is needed once things are under way—that, indeed, things can get terribly snarled up and still go on running. If one studies a factory, an army group, or other large organization, one wonders how things get done at all, with the lack of leadership and with all the feather bedding. Perhaps they get done because we are still trading on our reserves of inner-direction, especially in the lower ranks. At any rate, the fact they do get done is no proof that there is someone in charge.

There are, of course, still some veto groups that have more power than others and some individuals who have more power than others. But the determination of who these are has to be made all over again for our time: we cannot be satisfied with the answers given by Marx, Mosca, Michels, Pareto, Weber, Veblen, or Burnham, though we can learn from all of them.

There are also phenomena in this vast country that evade all of them (and surely, too, evade my collaborators and me). One example is the immense power, both political and economic, possessed by Artie Samish, allegedly the veto-group boss of California. Samish is a new-type lobbyist, who represents not one but scores of interests, often competing ones, from truckers to chiropractors, and who plays one veto group off against others to shake them down and strengthen his own power: he has learned how the other-orientation of the established veto groups will lead them to call still other groups into being through his auspices. Since the old-line parties have little power in California, there is no way of reaching a clear-cut decision for or against a particular veto group through the party system; instead, the state officials have become dependent on Samish for electoral support, or at least non-opposition, through his herded groups of voters and their cash contributions; moreover, he knows how to go directly to the people through the "democratic" plebiscite machinery.[4]

Carey McWilliams has observed that Samish's power rests both on the peculiar election machinery of the state and on the fact that no one industry or allied group of industries, no one union, one ethnic

---

[4] Ironically enough, but typically enough, Samish craves the one power he does not have: social power in the society-page sense. A poor boy in origin, he can make or break businessmen and politicians but cannot get into the more exclusive clubs. And while consciously he is said to despise these social leaders whom he can so easily frighten and manipulate, he cannot purge himself of the childhood hurts and childhood images of power that make him vulnerable to their exclusion of him. In this, of course, he resembles other and better-known dictators.

I have drawn on Carey McWilliams, "Guy Who Gets Things Done," *Nation* (1949), 31–33; and Lester Velie, "Secret Boss of California," *Collier's* (August 13, 20, 1949), 11–13, 12–13.

group or region, is dominant. The situation is very different in a state like Montana, where copper is pivotal, and one must be either for the union or for Anaconda. It is different again in Virginia where, as V. O. Key shows in *Southern Politics*, the setup of the state constitution favors control by the old courthouse crowd. In view of these divergences, rooted in local legal niceties as well as in major social and economic factors, it is apparent that any discussion of class and power on the national scene can at best be only an approximation. Yet I would venture to say that the United States is on the whole more like California in its variety—but without its veto boss—than like Montana and Virginia in their particularity. The vaster number of veto groups, and their greater power, mean that no one man or small group of men can amass the power nationally that Artie Samish and, in earlier days, Huey Long, have held locally.

Rather, power on the national scene must be viewed in terms of issues. It is possible that, where an issue involves only two or three groups, themselves tiny minorities, the official or unofficial broker among the groups can be quite powerful—but only on that issue. However, where the issue involves the country as a whole, no individual or group leadership is likely to be very effective, because the entrenched veto groups cannot be budged: unlike a party that may be defeated at the polls, or a class that may be replaced by another class, the veto groups are always "in."

One might ask whether one would not find, over a long period of time, that decisions in America favored one group or class—thereby, by definition, the ruling group or class—over others. Does not wealth exert its pull in the long run? In the past this has been so; for the future I doubt it. The future seems to be in the hands of the small business and professional men who control Congress, such as realtors, lawyers, car salesmen, undertakers, and so on; of the military men who control defense and, in part, foreign policy; of the big-business managers and their lawyers, finance-committee men, and other counselors who decide on plant investment and influence the rate of technological change; of the labor leaders who control worker productivity and worker votes; of the black-belt whites who have the greatest stake in southern politics; of the Poles, Italians, Jews, and Irishmen who have stakes in foreign policy, city jobs, and ethnic, religious and cultural organizations; of the editorializers and storytellers who help socialize the young, tease and train the adult, and amuse and annoy the aged; of the farmers—themselves a warring congeries of cattlemen, corn men, dairymen, cotton men, and so on—who control key departments and committees and who, as the living representatives of our inner-directed past, control many of our memories; of the Russians and, to a lesser degree, other foreign powers who control much of our agenda of attention; and so on. The reader can complete the list. Power in America seems to me situational and mercurial; it resists attempts to locate it the way a molecule, under the Heisenberg principle, resists attempts simultaneously to locate it and time its velocity.

But people are afraid of this indeterminacy and amorphousness in the cosmology of power. Even those intellectuals, for instance, who feel themselves very much out of power and who are frightened of those who they think have the power, prefer to be scared by the power structures they conjure up than to face the possibility that the power structure they believe exists has largely evaporated. Most people prefer to suffer with interpretations that give their world meaning than to relax in the cave without an Ariadne's thread.

The Higher Circles*

C. Wright Mills

C. Wright Mills, the late Columbia University sociologist and author of several noted studies (*White Collar* and *The Power Elite* among others) discusses here the patterns of interrelationship between the veto groups and major governmental agencies. Mills registers his concern with the threat of publicly non-responsive power in these elites. He calls attention to the consequences that interlocking power groups have for the whole idea of citizen participation, which is at the base of democratic theory.

The powers of ordinary men are circumscribed by the everyday worlds in which they live, yet even in these rounds of job, family, and neighborhood they often seem driven by forces they can neither understand nor govern. "Great changes" are beyond their control, but affect their conduct and outlook none the less. The very framework of modern society confines them to projects not their own, but from every side, such changes now press upon the men and women of the mass society, who accordingly feel that they are without purpose in an epoch in which they are without power.

*From *The Power Elite* by C. Wright Mills. Copyright © 1956 by Oxford University Press, Inc. Reprinted by permission.

But not all men are in this sense ordinary. As the means of information and of power are centralized, some men come to occupy positions in American society from which they can look down upon, so to speak, and by their decisions mightily affect, the everyday worlds of ordinary men and women. They are not made by their jobs; they set up and break down jobs for thousands of others; they are not confined by simple family responsibilities; they can escape. They may live in many hotels and houses, but they are bound by no one community. They need not merely "meet the demands of the day and hour"; in some part, they create these demands, and cause others to meet them. Whether or not they profess their power, their technical and political experience of it far transcends that of the underlying population. What Jacob Burckhardt said of "great men," most Americans might well say of their elite: "They are all that we are not."[1]

The power elite is composed of men whose positions enable them to transcend the ordinary environments of ordinary men and women; they are in positions to make decisions having major consequences. Whether they do or do not make such decisions is less important than the fact that they do occupy such pivotal positions: their failure to act, their failure to make decisions, is itself an act that is often of greater consequence than the decisions they do make. For they are in command of the major hierarchies and organizations of modern society. They rule the big corporations. They run the machinery of the state and claim its prerogatives. They direct the military establishment. They occupy the strategic command posts of the social structure, in which are now centered the effective means of the power and the wealth and the celebrity which they enjoy.

The power elite are not solitary rulers. Advisers and consultants, spokesmen and opinion-makers are often the captains of their higher thought and decision. Immediately below the elite are the professional politicians of the middle levels of power, in the Congress and in the pressure groups, as well as among the new and old upper classes of town and city and region. Mingling with them, in curious ways which we shall explore, are those professional celebrities who live by being continually displayed but are never, so long as they remain celebrities, displayed enough. If such celebrities are not at the head of any dominating hierarchy, they do often have the power to distract the attention of the public or afford sensations to the masses, or, more directly, to gain the ear of those who do occupy positions of direct power. More

---

[1] Jacob Burckhardt, *Force and Freedom* (New York: Pantheon Books, 1943), pp. 303 ff.

or less unattached, as critics of morality and technicians of power, as spokesmen of God and creators of mass sensibility, such celebrities and consultants are part of the immediate scene in which the drama of the elite is enacted. But that drama itself is centered in the command posts of the major institutional hierarchies.

I

The truth about the nature and the power of the elite is not some secret which men of affairs know but will not tell. Such men hold quite various theories about their own roles in the sequence of event and decision. Ofter they are uncertain about their roles, and even more often they allow their fears and their hopes to affect their assessment of their own power. No matter how great their actual power, they tend to be less acutely aware of it than of the resistances of others to its use. Moreover, most American men of affairs have learned well the rhetoric of public relations, in some cases even to the point of using it when they are alone, and thus coming to believe it. The personal awareness of the actors is only one of the several sources one must examine in order to understand the higher circles. Yet many who believe that there is no elite, or at any rate none of any consequence, rest their argument upon what men of affairs believe about themselves, or at least assert in public.

There is, however, another view: those who feel, even if vaguely, that a compact and powerful elite of great importance does now prevail in America often base that feeling upon the historical trend of our time. They have felt, for example, the domination of the military event, and from this they infer that generals and admirals, as well as other men of decision influenced by them, must be enormously powerful. They hear that the Congress has again abdicated to a handful of men decisions clearly related to the issue of war or peace. They know that the bomb was dropped over Japan in the name of the United States of America, although they were at no time consulted about the matter. They feel that they live in a time of big decisions; they know that they are not making any. Accordingly, as they consider the present as history, they infer that at its center, making decisions or failing to make them, there must be an elite power.

On the one hand, those who share this feeling about big historical events assume that there is an elite and that its power is great. On the other hand, those who listen carefully to the reports of men apparently involved in the great decisions often do not believe that there is an elite whose powers are of decisive consequence.

Both views must be taken into account, but neither is adequate. The way to understand the power of the American elite lies neither solely in recognizing the historic scale of events nor in accepting the personal awareness reported by men of apparent decision. Behind such men and behind the events of history, linking the two, are the major institutions of modern society. These hierarchies of state and corporation and army constitute the means of power; as such they are now of a consequence not before equaled in human history—and at their summits, there are now those command posts of modern society which offer us the sociological key to an understanding of the role of the higher circles in America.

Within American society, major national power now resides in the economic, the political, and the military domains. Other institutions seem off to the side of modern history, and, on occasion, duly subordinated to these. No family is as directly powerful in national affairs as any major corporation; no church is as directly powerful in the external biographies of young men in America today as the military establishment; no college is as powerful in the shaping of momentous events as the National Security Council. Religious, educational, and family institutions are not autonomous centers of national power; on the contrary, these decentralized areas are increasingly shaped by the big three, in which developments of decisive and immediate consequence now occur.

Families and churches and schools adapt to modern life; governments and armies and corporations shape it; and, as they do so, they turn these lesser institutions into means for their ends. Religious institutions provide chaplains to the armed forces where they are used as a means of increasing the effectiveness of its morale to kill. Schools select and train men for their jobs in corporations and their specialized tasks in the armed forces. The extended family has, of course, long been broken up by the industrial revolution, and now the son and the father are removed from the family, by compulsion if need be, whenever the army of the state sends out the call. And the symbols of all these lesser institutions are used to legitimate the power and the decisions of the big three.

The life–fate of the modern individual depends not only upon the family into which he was born or which he enters by marriage, but increasingly upon the corporation in which he spends the most alert hours of his best years; not only upon the school where he is educated as a child and adolescent, but also upon the state which touches him throughout his life; not only upon the church in which on occasion he hears the word of God, but also upon the army in which he is disciplined.

If the centralized state could not rely upon the inculcation of nationalist loyalties in public and private schools, its leaders would promptly seek to modify the decentralized educational system. If the bankruptcy rate among the top five hundred corporations were as high as the general divorce rate among the thirty-seven million married couples, there would be economic catastrophe on an international scale. If members of armies gave to them no more of their lives than do believers to the churches to which they belong, there would be a military crisis.

Within each of the big three, the typical institutional unit has become enlarged, has become administrative, and, in the power of its decisions, has become centralized. Behind these developments there is a fabulous technology, for as institutions they have incorporated this technology and guide it, even as it shapes and paces their developments.

The economy—once a great scatter of small productive units in autonomous balance—has become dominated by two or three hundred giant corporations, administratively and politically interrelated, which together hold the keys to economic decisions.

The political order, once a decentralized set of several dozen states with a weak spinal cord, has become a centralized, executive establishment which has taken up into itself many powers previously scattered, and now enters into each and every cranny of the social structure.

The military order, once a slim establishment in a context of distrust fed by state militia, has become the largest and most expensive feature of government, and, although well versed in smiling public relations, now has all the grim and clumsy efficiency of a sprawling bureaucratic domain.

In each of these institutional areas, the means of power at the disposal of decision makers have increased enormously; their central executive powers have been enhanced; within each of them modern administrative routines have been elaborated and tightened up.

As each of these domains becomes enlarged and centralized, the consequences of its activities become greater, and its traffic with the others increases. The decisions of a handful of corporations bear upon military and political as well as upon economic developments around the world. The decisions of the military establishment rest upon and grievously affect political life as well as the very level of economic activity. The decisions made within the political domain determine economic activities and military programs. There is no longer, on the one hand, an economy, and, on the other hand, a political order containing a military establishment unimportant to politics and to money-making. There is a political economy linked, in a thousand ways, with military institutions and decisions. On each side of the world–split running through central Europe and around the Asiatic rimlands, there is an ever increasing interlocking of economic, military, and political structures.[2] If there is government intervention in the corporate economy, so is there corporate intervention in the governmental process. In the structural sense, this triangle of power is the source of the interlocking directorate that is most important for the historical structure of the present.

The fact of the interlocking is clearly revealed at each of the points of crisis of modern capitalistic society—slump, war, and boom. In each, men of decision are led to an awareness of the interdependence of the major institutional orders. In the nineteenth century, when the scale of all institutions was smaller, their liberal integration was achieved in the automatic economy by an autonomous play of market forces, and in the automatic political domain by the bargain and the vote. It was then assumed that out of the imbalance and friction that followed the limited decisions than possible a new equilibrium would in due course emerge. That can no longer be assumed, and it is not assumed by the men at the top of each of the three dominant hierarchies.

For given the scope of their consequences, decisions—and indecisions—in any one of these ramify into the others, and hence top decisions tend either to become coordinated or to lead to a commanding indecision. It has not always been like this. When numerous small entrepreneurs made up the economy, for example, many of them could fail and the consequences still remain local; political and military authorities did not intervene. But now, given political expectations and military commitments, can they afford to allow key units of the private corporate economy to break down in slump? Increasingly, they do intervene in economic affairs, and as they do so, the controlling decisions in each order are inspected by agents of the other two, and economic, military, and political structures are interlocked.

---

[2] See Hans Gerth and C. Wright Mills, *Character and Social Structure* (New York: Harcourt, Brace & World, 1953), pp. 457 ff.

At the pinnacle of each of the three enlarged and centralized domains, there have arisen those higher circles which make up the economic, the political, and the military elites. At the top of the economy, among the corporate rich, there are the chief executives; at the top of the political order, the members of the political directorate; at the top of the military establishment, the elite of soldier–statesmen clustered in and around the Joint Chiefs of Staff and the upper echelon. As each of these domains has coincided with the others, as decisions tend to become total in their consequence, the leading men in each of the three domains of power—the warlords, the corporation chieftains, the political directorate—tend to come together, to form the power elite of America.

II

The higher circles in and around these command posts are often thought of in terms of what their members possess: they have a greater share than other people of the things and experiences that are most highly valued. From this point of view, the elite are simply those who have the most of what there is to have, which is generally held to include money, power, and prestige—as well as all the ways of life to which these lead.[3] But the elite are not simply those who have the most, for they could not "have the most" were it not for their positions in the great institutions. For such institutions are the necessary bases of power, of wealth, and of prestige, and at the same time, the chief means of exercising power, of acquiring and retaining wealth, and of cashing in the higher claims for prestige.

By the powerful we mean, of course, those who are able to realize their will, even if others resist it. No one, accordingly, can be truly powerful unless he has access to the command of major institutions, for it is over these institutional means of power that the truly powerful are, in the first instance, powerful. Higher politicians and key officials of government command such institutional power, so do admirals and generals, and so do the major owners and executives of

---

[3]The statistical idea of choosing some value and calling those who have the most of it an elite derives, in modern times, from the Italian economist, Pareto, who puts the central point in this way: "Let us assume that in every branch of human activity each individual is given an index which stands as a sign of his capacity, very much the way grades are given in the various subjects in examinations in school. . . . So let us make a class of people who have the highest indices in their branch of activity, and to that class give the name of *elite*." Vilfredo Pareto, *The Mind and Society* (New York: Harcourt, Brace, 1935), par. 2027 and 2031. . . .

the larger corporations. Not all power, it is true, is anchored in and exercised by means of such institutions, but only within and through them can power be more or less continuous and important.

Wealth also is acquired and held in and through institutions. The pyramid of wealth cannot be understood merely in terms of the very rich; for the great inheriting families, as we shall see, are now supplemented by the corporate institutions of modern society: every one of the very rich families has been and is closely connected—always legally and frequently managerially as well—with one of the multi-million dollar corporations.

The modern corporation is the prime source of wealth, but, in latter-day capitalism, the political apparatus also opens and closes many avenues to wealth. The amount as well as the source of income, the power over consumer's goods as well as over productive capital, are determined by position within the political economy. If our interest in the very rich goes beyond their lavish or their miserly consumption, we must examine their relations to modern forms of corporate property as well as to the state; for such relations now determine the chances of men to secure big property and to receive high income.

Great prestige increasingly follows the major institutional units of the social structure. It is obvious that prestige depends, often quite decisively, upon access to the publicity machines that are now a central and normal feature of all the big institutions of modern America. Moreover, one feature of these hierarchies of corporation, state, and military establishment is that their top positions are increasingly interchangeable. One result of this is the accumulative nature of prestige. Claims for prestige, for example, may be initially based on military roles, then expressed in and augmented by an educational institution run by corporate executives, and cashed in, finally, in the political order, where, for General Eisenhower and those he represents, power and prestige finally meet at the very peak. Like wealth and power, prestige tends to be cumulative; the more of it you have, the more you can get. These values also tend to be translatable into one another: the wealthy find it easier than the poor to gain power; those with status find it easier than those without it to control opportunities for wealth.

If we took the one hundred most powerful men in America, the one hundred wealthiest, and the one hundred most celebrated away from the institutional positions they now occupy, away from their resources of men and women and money, away from the media of mass communication that are now focused upon them—then they would be powerless and poor and uncelebrated. For power is not of a man. Wealth does not center in the person of the wealthy. Celebrity is not inherent in any personality. To be celebrated, to be wealthy, to have power requires access to major institutions, for the institutional positions men occupy determine in large part their chances to have and to hold these valued experiences.

III

The people of the higher circles may also be conceived as members of a top social stratum, as a set of groups whose members know one another, see one another socially and at business, and so, in making decisions, take one another into account. The elite, according to this conception, feel themselves to be, and are felt by others to be, the inner circle of "the upper social classes."[4] They form a more or less compact social and psychological entity; they have become self-conscious members of a social class. People are either accepted into this class or they are not, and there is a qualitative split, rather than merely a numerical scale, separating them from those who are not elite. They are more or less aware of themselves as a social class and they behave toward one another differently from the way they do toward members of other classes. They accept one another, understand one another, marry one another, tend to work and to think if not together at least alike.

Now, we do not want by our definition to prejudge whether the elite of the command posts are conscious members of such a socially recognized class, or whether considerable proportions of the elite derive from such a clear and distinct class. These are matters to be

---

[4] The conception of the elite as members of a top social stratum, is, of course, in line with the prevailing common-sense view of stratification. Technically, it is closer to "status group" than to "class," and has been very well stated by Joseph A. Schumpeter, "Social Classes in an Ethically Homogeneous Environment," *Imperialism and Social Classes* (New York: Augustus M. Kelley, Inc., 1951, pp. 133 ff., especially pp. 137–47. Cf. also his *Capitalism, Socialism and Democracy*, 3rd ed. (New York: Harper, 1950), Part II. For the distinction between class and status groups, see *From Max Weber: Essays in Sociology* (trans. and ed. by Gerth and Mills; New York: Oxford University Press, 1946). For an analysis of Pareto's conception of the elite compared with Marx's conception of classes, as well as data on France, see Raymond Aron, "Social Structure and Ruling Class," *British Journal of Sociology*, vol. I, nos. 1 and 2 (1950).

investigated. Yet in order to be able to recognize what we intend to investigate, we must note something that all biographies and memoirs of the wealthy and the powerful and the eminent make clear: no matter what else they may be, the people of these higher circles are involved in a set of overlapping "crowds" and intricately connected "cliques." There is a kind of mutual attraction among those who "sit on the same terrace"—although this often becomes clear to them, as well as to others, only at the point at which they feel the need to draw the line; only when, in their common defense, they come to understand what they have in common, and so close their ranks against outsiders.

The idea of such [a] ruling stratum implies that most of its members have similar social origins, that throughout their lives they maintain a network of informal connections, and that to some degree there is an interchangeability of position between the various hierarchies of money and power and celebrity. We must, of course, note at once that if such an elite stratum does exist, its social visibility and its form, for very solid historical reasons, are quite different from those of the noble cousinhoods that once ruled various European nations.

That American society has never passed through a feudal epoch is of decisive importance to the nature of the American elite, as well as to American society as a historic whole. For it means that no nobility or aristocracy established before the capitalist era has stood in tense opposition to the higher bourgeoisie. It means that this bourgeoisie has monopolized not only wealth but prestige and power as well. It means that no set of noble families has commanded the top positions and monopolized the values that are generally held in high esteem; and certainly that no set has done so explicitly by inherited right. It means that no high church dignitaries or court nobilities, no entranched landlords with honorific accouterments, no monopolists of high army posts have opposed the enriched bourgeoisie and in the name of birth and prerogative successfully resisted its self-making.

But this does *not* mean that there are no upper strata in the United States. That they emerged from a "middle class" that had no recognized aristocratic superiors does not mean they remained middle class when enormous increases in wealth made their own superiority possible. Their origins and their newness may have made the upper strata less visible in America than elsewhere. But in America today there are in fact tiers and ranges of wealth and power of which people in the middle and lower ranks know very little and may not even dream. There are families who, in their well-being, are quite insulated from the economic jolts and lurches felt by the merely prosperous and those farther down the scale. There are also men of power who in quite small groups make decisions of enormous consequence for the underlying population.

The American elite entered modern history as a virtually unopposed bourgeoisie. No national bourgeoisie, before or since, has had such opportunities and advantages. Having no military neighbors, they easily occupied an isolated continent stocked with natural resources and immensely inviting to a willing labor force. A framework of power and an ideology for its justification were already at hand. Against mercantilist restriction, they inherited the principle of laissez faire; against southern planters, they imposed the principle of industrialism. The Revolutionary War put an end to colonial pretensions to nobility, as loyalists fled the country and many estates were broken up. The Jacksonian upheaval with its status revolution put an end to pretensions to monopoly of descent by the old New England families. The Civil War broke the power, and so in due course the prestige, of the ante-bellum South's claimants for the higher esteem. The tempo of the whole capitalist development made it impossible for an inherited nobility to develop and endure in America.

No fixed ruling class, anchored in agrarian life and coming to flower in military glory, could contain in America the historic thrust of commerce and industry, or subordinate to itself the capitalist elite —as capitalists were subordinated, for example, in Germany and Japan. Nor could such a ruling class anywhere in the world contain that of the United States when industrialized violence came to decide history. Witness the fate of Germany and Japan in the two world wars of the twentieth century; and indeed the fate of Britain herself and her model ruling class, as New York became the inevitable economic, and Washington the inevitable political capital of the Western capitalist world.

IV

The elite who occupy the command posts may be seen as the possessors of power and wealth and celebrity; they may be seen as members of the upper stratum of a capitalistic society. They may also be defined in terms of psychological and moral criteria as certain kinds of selected individuals. So defined, the elite, quite simply, are people of superior character and energy.

The humanist, for example, may conceive of the "elite" not as a social level or category, but as a scatter of those individuals who attempt to transcend themselves, and accordingly, are more noble, more efficient, made out of better stuff. It does not matter whether they are poor or rich, whether they hold high position or low, whether they are acclaimed or despised; they are elite because of the kind of individuals they are. The rest of the population is mass, which, according to this conception, sluggishly relaxes into uncomfortable mediocrity.[5]

This is the sort of socially unlocated conception which some American writers with conservative yearnings have recently sought to develop. But most moral and psychological conceptions of the elite are much less sophisticated, concerning themselves not with individuals but with the stratum as a whole. Such ideas, in fact, always arise in a society in which some people possess more than do others of what there is to possess. People with advantages are loath to believe that they just happen to be people with advantages. They come readily to define themselves as inherently worthy of what they possess; they come to believe themselves "naturally" elite; and, in fact, to imagine their possessions and their privileges as natural extensions of their own elite selves. In this sense, the idea of the elite as composed of men and women having a finer moral character is an ideology of the elite as a privileged ruling stratum, and this is true whether the ideology is elite made or made up for it by others.

In eras of equalitarian rhetoric, the more intelligent or the more articulate among the lower and middle classes, as well as guilty members of the upper, may come to entertain ideas of a counter-elite. In Western society, as a matter of fact, there is a long tradition and varied images of the poor, the exploited, and the oppressed as the truly virtuous, the wise, and the blessed. Stemming from Christian tradition, this moral idea of a counter-elite, composed of essentially higher types condemned to a lowly station, may be and has been used by the underlying population to justify harsh criticism of ruling elites and to celebrate utopian images of a new elite to come.

The moral conception of the elite, however, is not always merely an ideology of the overprivileged or a counter-ideology of the under-

---

[5] The most popular essay in recent years which defines the elite and the mass in terms of a morally evaluated character-type is probably José Ortega y Gasset's, *The Revolt of the Masses*, 1932 (New York: New American Library, Mentor Edition, 1950), esp. pp. 91 ff.

privileged. It is often a fact: having controlled experiences and select privileges, many individuals of the upper stratum do come in due course to approximate the types of character they claim to embody. Even when we give up—as we must—the idea that the elite man or woman is born with an elite character, we need not dismiss the idea that their experiences and trainings develop in them characters of a specific type.

Nowadays we must qualify the idea of elite as composed of higher types of individuals, for the men who are selected for and shaped by the top positions have many spokesmen and advisers and ghosts and make-up men who modify their self-conceptions and create their public images, as well as shape many of their decisions. There is, of course, considerable variation among the elite in this respect, but as a general rule in America today, it would be naïve to interpret any major elite group merely in terms of its ostensible personnel. The American elite often seems less a collection of persons than of corporate entities, which are in great part created and spoken for as standard types of "personality." Even the most apparently free-lance celebrity is usually a sort of synthetic production turned out each week by a disciplined staff which systematically ponders the effect of the easy ad-libbed gags the celebrity "spontaneously" echoes.

Yet, in so far as the elite flourishes as a social class or as a set of men at the command posts, it will select and form certain types of personality, and reject others. The kind of moral and psychological beings men become is in large part determined by the values they experience and the institutional roles they are allowed and expected to play. From the biographer's point of view, a man of the upper classes is formed by his relations with others like himself in a series of small intimate groupings through which he passes and to which throughout his lifetime he may return. So conceived, the elite is a set of higher circles whose members are selected, trained and certified and permitted intimate access to those who command the impersonal institutional hierarchies of modern society. If there is any one key to the *psychological* idea of the elite, it is that they combine in their persons an awareness of impersonal decision-making with intimate sensibilities shared with one another. To understand the elite as a social class we must examine a whole series of smaller face-to-face milieux, the most obvious of which, historically, has been the upper-class family, but the most important of which today are the proper secondary school and the metropolitan club.

V

These several notions of the elite, when appropriately understood, are intricately bound up with one another, and we shall use them all in this examination of American success. We shall study each of several higher circles as offering candidates for the elite, and we shall do so in terms of the major institutions making up the total society of America; within and between each of these institutions, we shall trace the interrelations of wealth and power and prestige. But our main concern is with the power of those who now occupy the command posts, and with the role which they are enacting in the history of our epoch.

Such an elite may be conceived as omnipotent, and its powers thought of as a great hidden design. Thus, in vulgar Marxism, events and trends are explained by reference to "the will of the bourgeoisie"; in Nazism, by reference to "the conspiracy of the Jews"; by the petty Right in America today, by reference to "the hidden force" of Communist spies. According to such notions of the omnipotent elite as historical cause, the elite is never an entirely visible agency. It is, in fact, a secular substitute for the will of God, being realized in a sort of providential design, except that usually non-elite men are thought capable of opposing it and eventually overcoming it.

The opposite view—of the elite as impotent—is now quite popular among liberal-minded observers. Far from being omnipotent, the elites are thought to be so scattered as to lack any coherence as a historical force. Their invisibility is not the invisibility of secrecy but the invisibility of the multitude. Those who occupy the formal places of authority are so checkmated—by other elites exerting pressure, or by the public as an electorate, or by constitutional codes—that, although there may be upper classes, there is no ruling class; although there may be men of power, there is no power elite; although there may be a system of stratification, it has no effective top. In the extreme, this view of the elite, as weakened by compromise and disunited to the point of nullity, is a substitute for impersonal collective fate; for, in this view, the decisions of the visible men of the higher circles do not count in history.

Internationally, the image of the omnipotent elite tends to prevail. All good events and pleasing happenings are quickly imputed by the opinion-makers to the leaders of their own nation; all bad events and unpleasant experiences are imputed to the enemy abroad. In both cases, the omnipotence of evil rulers or of virtuous leaders is assumed. Within the nation, the use of such rhetoric is rather more complicated: when men speak of the power of their own party or circle, they and their leaders are, of course, impotent; only "the people" are omnipotent. But, when they speak of the power of their opponent's party or circle, they impute to them omnipotence; "the people" are now powerlessly taken in.

More generally, American men of power tend, by convention, to deny that they are powerful. No American runs for office in order to rule or even govern, but only to serve; he does not become a bureaucrat or even an official, but a public servant. And nowadays, as I have already pointed out, such postures have become standard features of the public-relations programs of all men of power. So firm a part of the style of power-wielding have they become that conservative writers readily misinterpret them as indicating a trend toward an "amorphous power situation."

But the "power situation" of America today is less amorphous than is the perspective of those who see it as a romantic confusion. It is less a flat, momentary "situation" than a graded, durable structure. And if those who occupy its top grades are not omnipotent, neither are they impotent. It is the form and the height of the gradation of power that we must examine if we would understand the degree of power held and exercised by the elite.

If the power to decide such national issues as are decided were shared in an absolutely equal way, there would be no power elite; in fact, there would be no *gradation* of power, but only a radical homogeneity. At the opposite extreme as well, if the power to decide issues were absolutely monopolized by one small group, there would be no gradation of power; there would simply be this small group in command, and below it, the undifferentiated, dominated masses. American society today represents neither the one nor the other of these extremes, but a conception of them is none the less useful: it makes us realize more clearly the question of the structure of power in the United States and the position of the power elite within it.

Within each of the most powerful institutional orders of modern society there is a gradation of power. The owner of a roadside fruit stand does not have as much power in any area of social or economic or political decision as the head of a multi-million-dollar fruit corporation; no lieutenant on the line is as powerful as the chief of staff in the Pentagon; no deputy sheriff carries as much authority as the president of the United States. Accordingly, the problem of defining the power elite concerns the level at which we wish to draw the line. By lowering the line, we could define the elite out of existence; by raising it, we could make the elite a very small circle indeed. In a preliminary and minimum way, we draw the line crudely, in charcoal as it were: By the power elite, we refer to those political, economic, and military circles which as an intricate set of overlapping cliques share decisions having at least national consequences. In so far as national events are decided, the power elite are those who decide them.

To say that there are obvious gradations of power and of opportunities to decide within modern society is not to say that the powerful are united, that they fully know what they do, or that they are consciously joined in conspiracy. Such issues are best faced if we concern ourselves, in the first instance, more with the structural position of the high and mighty, and with the consequences of their decisions, than with the extent of their awareness or the purity of their motives. To understand the power elite, we must attend to three major keys:

1. One, which we shall emphasize throughout our discussion of each of the higher circles, is the psychology of the several elites in their respective milieux. In so far as the power elite is composed of men of similar origin and education, in so far as their careers and their styles of life are similar, there are psychological and social bases for their unity, resting upon the fact that they are of similar social type and leading to the fact of their easy intermingling. This kind of unity reaches its frothier apex in the sharing of that prestige that is to be had in the world of the celebrity; it achieves a more solid culmination in the fact of the interchangeability of positions within and between the three dominant institutional orders.

2. Behind such psychological and social unity as we may find, are the structure and the mechanics of those institutional hierarchies over which the political directorate, the corporate rich, and the high military now preside. The greater the scale of these bureaucratic domains, the greater the scope of their respective elite's power. How each of the major hierarchies is shaped and what relations it has with the other hierarchies determine in large part the relations of their rulers. If these hierarchies are scattered and disjointed, then their respective elites tend to be scattered and disjointed; if they have many interconnections and points of coinciding interest, then their elites tend to form a coherent kind of grouping.

The unity of the elite is not a simple reflection of the unity of institutions, but men and institutions are always related, and our conception of the power elite invites us to determine that relation. Today in America there are several important structural coincidences of interest between these institutional domains, including the development of a permanent war establishment by a privately incorporated economy inside a political vacuum.

3. The unity of the power elite, however, does not rest solely on psychological similarity and social intermingling, nor entirely on the structural coincidences of commanding positions and interests. At times it is the unity of a more explicit coordination. To say that these three higher circles are increasingly coordinated, that this is *one* basis of their unity, and that at times—as during the wars—such coordination is quite decisive, is not to say that the coordination is total or continuous, or even that it is very surefooted. Much less is it to say that willful coordination is the sole or the major basis of their unity, or that the power elite has emerged as the realization of a plan. But it is to say that as the institutional mechanics of our time have opened up avenues to men pursuing their several interests, many of them have come to see that these several interests could be realized more easily if they worked together, in informal as well as in more formal ways, and accordingly they have done so.

VI

It is not my thesis that for all epochs of human history and in all nations, a creative minority, a ruling class, an omnipotent elite, shapes all historical events. Such statements, upon careful examination, usually turn out to be mere tautologies,[6] and even when they are not, they are so entirely general as to be useless in the attempt to understand the history of the present. The minimum definition of the power elite as those who decide whatever is decided of major consequence, does not imply that the members of this elite are always and necessarily the history-makers; neither does it imply that they never are. We must not confuse the conception of the elite, which we wish to define, with one theory about their role:

---

[6]As in the case, quite notably, of Gaetano Mosca, *The Ruling Class* (New York: McGraw-Hill, 1939). For a sharp analysis of Mosca, see Fritz Morstein Marx, "The Bureaucratic State," *Review of Politics*, I (1939), 457 ff. See also Mills, "On Intellectual Craftsmanship" (April, 1952); mimeographed, Columbia College, February, 1965.

that they are the history-makers of our time. To define the elite, for example, as "those who rule America" is less to define a conception than to state one hypothesis about the role and power of that elite. No matter how we might define the elite, the extent of its members' power is subject to historical variation. If, in a dogmatic way, we try to include that variation in our generic definition, we foolishly limit the use of a needed conception. If we insist that the elite be defined as a strictly coordinated class that continually and absolutely rules, we are closing off from our view much to which the term more modestly defined might open to our observation. In short, our definition of the power elite cannot properly contain dogma concerning the degree and kind of power that ruling groups everywhere have. Much less should it permit us to smuggle into our discussion a theory of history.

During most of human history, historical change has not been visible to the people who were involved in it, or even to those enacting it. Ancient Egypt and Mesopotamia, for example, endured for some four hundred generations with but slight changes in their basic structure. That is six and a half times as long as the entire Christian era, which has only prevailed some sixty generations; it is about eighty times as long as the five generations of the United States' existence. But now the tempo of change is so rapid, and the means of observation so accessible, that the interplay of event and decision seems often to be quite historically visible, if we will only look carefully and from an adequate vantage point.

When knowledgeable journalists tell us that "events, not men, shape the big decisions," they are echoing the theory of history as Fortune, Chance, Fate, or the work of The Unseen Hand. For *events* is merely a modern word for these older ideas, all of which separate men from history-making, because all of them lead us to believe that history goes on behind men's backs. History is drift with no mastery; within it there is action but no deed; history is mere happening and the event intended by no one.[7]

The course of events in our time depends more on a series of human decisions than on any inevitable fate. The sociological meaning of *fate* is simply this: that when the decisions are innumerable and each one is of small consequence all of them add up in a way no man intended—to history as fate. But not all epochs are equally fateful. As the circle of those who decide is narrowed,

---

[7] See Karl Löwith, *Meaning in History* (Chicago: University of Chicago Press, 1949), pp. 125 ff. for concise and penetrating statements of several leading philosophies of history.

as the means of decision are centralized and the consequences of decisions become enormous, then the course of great events often rests upon the decisions of determinable circles. This does not necessarily mean that the same circle of men follow through from one event to another in such a way that all of history is merely their plot. The power of the elite does not necessarily mean that history is not also shaped by a series of small decisions, none of which are thought out. It does not mean that a hundred small arrangements and compromises and adaptations may not be built into the going policy and the living event. The idea of the power elite implies nothing about the process of decision-making as such: it is an attempt to delimit the social areas within which that process, whatever its character, goes on. It is a conception of who is involved in the process.

The degree of foresight and control of those who are involved in decisions that count may also vary. The idea of the power elite does not mean that the estimations and calculated risks upon which decisions are made are not often wrong and that the consequences are sometimes, indeed often, not those intended. Often those who make decisions are trapped by their own inadequacies and blinded by their own errors.

Yet in our time the pivotal moment does arise, and at that moment, small circles do decide or fail to decide. In either case, they are an elite of power. The dropping of the A-bombs over Japan was such a moment; the decision on Korea was such a moment; the confusion about Quemoy and Matsu, as well as before Dienbienphu were such moments; the sequence of maneuvers which involved the United States in World War II was such a "moment." Is it not true that much of the history of our times is composed of such moments? And is not that what is meant when it is said that we live in a time of big decisions, of decisively centralized power?

Most of us do not try to make sense of our age by believing in a Greek-like, eternal recurrence, nor by a Christian belief in a salvation to come, nor by any steady march of human progress. Even though we do not reflect upon such matters, the chances are we believe with Burckhardt that we live in a mere succession of events; that sheer continuity is the only principle of history. History is merely one thing after another; history is meaningless in that it is not the realization of any determinate plot. It is true, of course, that our sense of continuity, our feeling for the history of our time, is affected by crisis. But we seldom look beyond the immediate crisis or the crisis felt to be just ahead. We believe neither in fate nor providence; and we assume, without talking about it, that "we"—as a nation—can decisively shape the future but that "we" as individuals somehow cannot do so.

Any meaning history has, "we" shall have to give to it by our actions. Yet the fact is that although we are all of us within history we do not all posses equal powers to make history. To pretend that we do is sociological nonsense and political irresponsibility. It is nonsense because any group or any individual is limited, first of all, by the technical and institutional means of power at its command; we do not all have equal access to the means of power that now exist, nor equal influence over their use. To pretend that "we" are all history-makers is politically irresponsible because it obfuscates any attempt to locate responsibility for the consequential decisions of men who do have access to the means of power.

From even the most superficial examination of the history of the Western society we learn that the power of decision-makers is first of all limited by the level of technique, by the *means* of power and violence and organization that prevail in a given society. In this connection we also learn that there is a fairly straight line running upward through the history of the West; that the means of oppression and exploitation, of violence and destruction, as well as the means of production and reconstruction, have been progressively enlarged and increasingly centralized.

As the institutional means of power and the means of communications that tie them together have become steadily more efficient, those now in command of them have come into command of instruments of rule quite unsurpassed in the history of mankind. And we are not yet at the climax of their development. We can no longer lean upon or take soft comfort from the historical ups and downs of ruling groups of previous epochs. In that sense, Hegel is correct: we learn from history that we cannot learn from it.

For every epoch and for every social structure, we must work out an answer to the question of the power of the elite. The ends of men are often merely hopes, but means are facts within some men's control. That is why all means of power tend to become ends to an elite that is in command of them. And that is why we may define the power elite in terms of the means of power—as those who occupy the command posts. The major questions about the American elite today—its composition, its unity, its power—must now be faced with due attention to the awesome means of power available to them. Caesar could do less with Rome than Napoleon with France; Napoleon less with France than Lenin with Russia;

and Lenin less with Russia than Hitler with Germany. But what was Caesar's power at its peak compared with the power of the changing inner circle of Soviet Russia or of America's temporary administrations? The men of either circle can cause great cities to be wiped out in a single night, and in a few weeks turn continents into thermonuclear wastelands. That the facilities of power are enormously enlarged and decisively centralized means that the decisions of small groups are now more consequential.

But to know that the top posts of modern social structures now permit more commanding decisions is not to know that the elite who occupy these posts are the history-makers. We might grant that the enlarged and integrated economic, military, and political structures are shaped to permit command decisions, yet still feel that, as it were, "they run themselves," that those who are on top, in short, are determined in their decisions by "necessity," which presumably means by the instituted roles that they play and the situation of these institutions in the total structure of society.

Do the elite determine the roles that they enact? Or do the roles that institutions make available to them determine the power of the elite? The general answer—and no general answer is sufficient —is that in different kinds of structures and epochs elites are quite differently related to the roles that they play: nothing in the nature of the elite or in the nature of history dictates an answer. It is also true that if most men and women take whatever roles are permitted to them and enact them as they are expected to by virtue of their position, this is precisely what the elite need *not* do, and often do not do. They may call into question the structure, their position within it, or the way in which they are to enact that position.

Nobody called for or permitted Napoleon to chase *Parlement* home on the *18 Brumaire*, and later to transform his consulate into an emperorship.[8] Nobody called for or permitted Adolf Hitler to proclaim himself "Leader and Chancellor" the day President Hindenburg died, to abolish and usurp roles by merging the presidency and the chancellorship. Nobody called for or permitted Franklin D. Roosevelt to make the series of decisions that led to the entrance of the United States into World War II. It was no "historical necessity," but a man named Truman who, with a few

---

[8] Some of these items are taken from Gerth and Mills, *Character and Social Structure*, pp. 405 ff. On role-determined and role-determining men, see also Sidney Hook's discussion, *The Hero in History* (New York: John Day Co., 1943).

other men, decided to drop a bomb on Hiroshima. It was no historical necessity, but an argument within a small circle of men that defeated Admiral Radford's proposal to bomb troops before Dienbienphu. Far from being dependent upon the structure of institutions, modern elites may smash one structure and set up another in which they then enact quite different roles. In fact, such destruction and creation of institutional structures, with all their means of power, when events seem to turn out well, is just what is involved in "great leadership," or, when they seem to turn out badly, great tyranny.

Some elite men *are*, of course, typically role-determined, but others are at times role-determining. They determine not only the role they play but today the roles of millions of other men. The creation of pivotal roles and their pivotal enactment occurs most readily when social structures are undergoing epochal transitions. It is clear that the international development of the United States to one of the two "great powers"—along with the new means of annihilation and administrative and psychic domination—have made of the United States in the middle years of the twentieth century precisely such an epochal pivot.

There is nothing about history that tells us that a power elite cannot make it. To be sure, the will of such men is always limited, but never before have the limits been so broad, for never before have the means of power been so enormous. It is this that makes our situation so precarious, and makes even more important an understanding of the powers and the limitations of the American elite. The problem of the nature and the power of this elite is now the only realistic and serious way to raise again the problem of responsible government.

VII

Those who have abandoned criticism for the new American celebration take readily to the view that the elite is impotent. If they were politically serious, they ought, on the basis of their view, to say to those presumably in charge of American policy:[9]

One day soon, you may believe that you have an opportunity to drop a bomb or a chance to exacerbate further your relations with

---

[9] I have taken the idea of the following kind of formulation from Joseph Wood Krutch's presentation of the morality of choice. See *The Measure of Man* (Indianapolis: Bobbs-Merrill Co., 1954), p. 52.

allies or with the Russians who might also drop it. But don't be so foolish as to believe that you really have a choice. You have neither choice nor chance. The whole Complex Situation of which you are merely one balancing part is the result of Economic and Social Forces, and so will be the fateful outcome. So stand by quietly, like Tolstoy's general, and let events proceed. Even if you did act, the consequences would not be what you intended, even if you had an intention.

But—if events come out well, talk as though you had decided. For then men have had moral choices and the power to make them and are, of course, responsible.

If events come out badly, say that *you* didn't have the real choice, and are, of course, not accountable: *they*, the others, had the choice and they are responsible. You can get away with this even though you have at your command half the world's forces and God knows how many bombs and bombers. For you are, in fact, an impotent item in the historical fate of your times; and moral responsibility is an illusion, although it is of great use if handled in a really alert public-relations manner.

The one implication that can be drawn from all such fatalisms is that if fortune or providence rules, then no elite of power can be justly considered a source of historical decisions, and the idea— much less the demand—of responsible leadership is an idle and an irresponsible notion. For clearly, an impotent elite, the plaything of history, cannot be held accountable. If the elite of our time do not have power, they cannot be held responsible; as men in a difficult position, they should engage our sympathies. The people of the United States are ruled by sovereign fortune; they, and with them their elite, are fatally overwhelmed by consequences they cannot control. If that is so, we ought all to do what many have in fact already done: withdraw entirely from political reflection and action into a materially comfortable and entirely private life.

If, on the other hand, we believe that war and peace and slump and prosperity are, precisely now, no longer matters of "fortune" or "fate," but that, precisely now more than ever, they are controllable, then we must ask—controllable by whom? The answer must be: By whom else but those who now command the enormously enlarged and decisively centralized means of decision and power? We may then ask: Why don't they, then? And for the answer to that, we must understand the context and the character of the American elite today.

There is nothing in the idea of the elite as impotent which should deter us from asking just such questions, which are now the most important questions political men can ask. The American elite is neither omnipotent nor impotent. These are abstract absolutes used publicly by spokesmen, as excuses or as boasts, but in terms of which we may seek to clarify the political issues before us, which just now are above all the issues of responsible power.

There is nothing in "the nature of history" *in our epoch* that rules out the pivotal function of small groups of decision-makers. On the contrary, the structure of the present is such as to make this not only a reasonable, but a rather compelling, view.

There is nothing in "the psychology of man," or in the social manner by which men are shaped and selected for and by the command posts of modern society, that makes unreasonable the view that they do confront choices and that the choices they make—or their failure to confront them—are history-making in their consequences.

Accordingly, political men now have every reason to hold the American power elite accountable for a decisive range of the historical events that make up the history of the present.

It is as fashionable, just now, to suppose that there is no power elite, as it was fashionable in the thirties to suppose a set of ruling-class villains to be the source of all social injustice and public malaise. I should be as far from supposing that some simple and unilateral ruling class could be firmly located as the prime mover of American society, as I should be from supposing that all historical change in America today is merely impersonal drift.

The view that all is blind drift is largely a fatalist projection of one's own feeling of impotence and perhaps, if one has ever been active politically in a principled way, a salve of one's guilt.

The view that all of history is due to the conspiracy of an easily located set of villains, or of heroes, is also a hurried projection from the difficult effort to understand how shifts in the structure of society open opportunities to various elites and how various elites take advantage or fail to take advantage of them. To accept either view— of all history as conspiracy or of all history as drift—is to relax the effort to understand the facts of power and the ways of the powerful.

VIII

In my attempt to discern the shape of the power elite of our time, and thus to give a responsible meaning to the anonymous

"They," which the underlying population opposes to the anonymous "We," I shall begin by briefly examining the higher elements which most people know best: the new and the old upper classes of local society and the metropolitan 400. I shall then outline the world of the celebrity, attempting to show that the prestige system of American society has now for the first time become truly national in scope; and that the more trivial and glamorous aspects of this national system of status tend at once to distract attention from its more authoritarian features and to justify the power that it often conceals.

In examining the very rich and the chief executives, I shall indicate how neither "America's Sixty Families" nor "The Managerial Revolution" provides an adequate idea of the transformation of the upper classes as they are organized today in the privileged stratum of the corporate rich.

After describing the American statesman as a historical type, I shall attempt to show that what observers in the Progressive Era called "the invisible government" has now become quite visible; and that what is usually taken to be the central content of politics, the pressures and the campaigns and the congressional maneuvering, has, in considerable part, now been relegated to the middle levels of power.

In discussing the military ascendancy, I shall try to make clear how it has come about that admirals and generals have assumed positions of decisive political and economic relevance, and how, in doing so, they have found many points of coinciding interests with the corporate rich and the political directorate of the visible government.

After these and other trends are made as plain as I can make them, I shall return to the master problems of the power elite, as well as take up the complementary notion of the mass society.

What I am asserting is that in this particular epoch a conjunction of historical circumstances has led to the rise of an elite of power; that the men of the circles composing this elite, severally and collectively, now make such key decisions as are made; and that, given the enlargement and the centralization of the means of power now available, the decisions that they make and fail to make carry more consequences for more people than has ever been the case in the world history of mankind.

I am also asserting that there has developed on the middle levels of power, a semi-organized stalemate, and that on the bottom level there has come into being a mass-like society which has little resemblance to the image of a society in which voluntary associations and classic publics hold the keys to power. The top of the American system of power is much more unified and much more powerful, the bottom is much more fragmented, and in truth, impotent, than is generally supposed by those who are distracted by the middling units of power which neither express such will as exists at the bottom nor determine the decisions at the top.

The Military–Industrial Complex*

Fred J. Cook

As Mills indicated in the preceding piece, a burgeoning military-industrial complex in the United States has become a cause for consternation among those who view the growth of a peacetime military establishment as a barrier to an American initiative in establishing the groundwork for peace in the world. Fred Cook, winner of the New York Newspaper Guild's Page One Award for three consecutive years, examines the relationship of the military to big business in his *Warfare State*, in which he documents the enormous increase of military influence on both domestic and foreign policy. In the following brief excerpt Cook summarizes the problem as it was enunciated by a concerned president, Dwight D. Eisenhower.

On the evening of January 17, 1961, President Dwight D. Eisenhower, in the tradition of George Washington, the predecessor with whom he liked most to be compared, appeared before the television cameras to make his farewell address to the American people. The great presidential seal flashed on television screens across the nation, and then the probing camera-eye turned its intense scrutiny upon the face, etched deeper now with lines of age and illness and care, of the man whom history will probably judge one of the best-loved, best-intentioned and least effectual of modern American presidents.

It was the innate good will and lofty intent of the man, his gift for rendering platitudes with a sincerity that made them seem

---

*Reprinted with permission of The Macmillan Company from *The Warfare State* by Fred J. Cook; © Fred J. Cook 1962.

momentous, that reached out to television audiences in moments such as this and touched some deep chord of affection in the hearts of the American people. The President, speaking now for the last time from the pinnacle of prestige and power of the world's most awesome elective office, began in characteristic terms. He recalled his fifty years of service to his country, his gratitude to those with whom he had worked in Congress and out, his desire in this moment of leave-taking to share "a few final thoughts with you, my countrymen," All this was characteristic Eisenhower, and it gave no hint of the uncharacteristic words to come—words of warning and of portent that would compose one of the most discussed messages in America in the years ahead.

The President approached the central theme of his speech by referring to the long Cold War that has divided Soviet Russia and the United States, that has split the world into camps of East and West. We were confronted, he said, by "a hostile ideology—global in scope, atheistic in character, ruthless in purpose and insidious in method." The danger it poses, he added, "promises to be of infinite duration." He warned his fellow countrymen that "a long and complex struggle" lay ahead; he recognized that the frustrations of such a struggle might lead to demands for drastic action, for the violence that seeks a quick and clear-cut victory; and he pleaded for the national self-control that would enable the American people to reject such counsels of rashness.

"Crises there will continue to be," he said. "In meeting them, whether foreign or domestic, great or small, there is a recurring temptation to feel that some spectacular and costly action could become the miraculous solution to all current difficulties."

But there were no such miraculous solutions. The great need of our times was for balance, restraint, the exercise of good and sober judgment. And so the President came to the core of his message.

Threats to democracy, "new in kind or degree," were constantly arising, and one of these, new both in kind and degree, Eisenhower proposed to discuss at length. He called it "the military–industrial complex," and he pictured it as a colossus that had come to dominate vast areas of American life.

"Until the latest of our world conflicts," he said,

the United States had no armaments industry. American makers of plowshares could, with time and as required, make swords as well.

But we can no longer risk emergency improvisation of national defense. We have been compelled to create a permanent armaments industry of vast proportions. Added to this, three and a half million men and women are directly engaged in the defense establishment. *We annually spend on military security alone more than the net income of all United States corporations.* [Italics added.]

Now this conjunction of an immense military establishment and a large arms industry is new in the American experience. *The total influence—economic, political, even spiritual—is felt in every city, every state house, every office of the federal government.* [Italics added.] We recognize the imperative need for this development. Yet we must not fail to comprehend its grave implications. Our toil, resources and livelihood are all involved; so is the very structure of our society.

In the councils of government, we must guard against the acquisition of unwarranted influence, whether sought or unsought, by the military–industrial complex. The potential for the disastrous rise of misplaced power exists and will persist.

We must never let the weight of this combination endanger our liberties or democratic processes. We should take nothing for granted. Only an alert and knowledgeable citizenry can compel the proper meshing of the huge industrial and military machinery of defense with our peaceful methods and goals, so that security and liberty may prosper together.

In these words, the outgoing President projected the issue. As he continued speaking, he developed it in greater depth. He stressed that a "technological revolution" had led to "sweeping changes in our industrial–military posture." The very complexity of this revolution had made intricate and costly research essential to national survival. The result had been that "the free university, historically the fountainhead of free ideas and scientific discovery, has experienced a revolution in the conduct of research. Partly because of the huge costs involved, a government contract becomes virtually a substitute for intellectual curiosity." The President feared "the prospect of domination of the nation's scholars by federal employment," and he feared, too—in words that suggested to some the haunting specter of Dr. Edward Teller, the so-called father of the H-bomb and the vociferous advocate of ever more powerful nuclear weapons—that dependence upon science would lead to a critical situation in which "public policy could itself become the captive of a scientific–technological elite."

Such was the *one warning*, the *one issue* Eisenhower stressed in his farewell words to the American people....

The Social–Industrial Complex*

Michael Harrington

Mutual cooperation between governmental agencies and private business is a continuing rather than an episodic affair. Michael Harrington, author of the startling expose of poverty in the United States, *The Other America,* in this article devotes his attention to tracing the developing patterns of alliance between private economic interests and that adjunct of the political system: education.

American business has long scrambled over the common good in its haste to pursue private profit. Industry's contribution to air pollution is only the most recent example of the consequences of this habit. But now the corporations proudly threaten a new, distinctive, and paradoxical danger. Instead of creating social problems, they are going to solve them. In a strangely optimistic speech at the University of Chicago last year [1966], Lyle M. Spencer, President of Science Research Associates (an IBM subsidiary), aptly and ominously named this new development the "social–industrial complex."

Spencer's enthusiasm is puzzling in that his phrase is modeled on one of the most somber statements Dwight Eisenhower ever made: his warning against the "military–industrial complex." And indeed, the phenomenon Spencer describes is quite similar to the united front of executives and generals which so alarmed President Eisenhower. The military–industrial complex bases itself on the war economy and a huge defense establishment. This enormous vested interest in the means of annihilation, Eisenhower feared, could subvert the democratic process on vital questions of war and peace. The social–industrial complex also builds upon public expenditure and a "partnership" between government and business. But its rationale is the Great Society, not the Cold War (much of the massive spending waits, in fact, upon the end of the tragic war in Vietnam).

As Spencer puts it, "Social causes which in the thirties were the domain of college professors, labor unions, and student demonstrations are today becoming the new business of business." What is menacing about this sudden outburst of corporate conscience is that satisfying social needs and making money are two distinct and often antagonistic undertakings. Certainly the urgent demands of the

---

*Copyright © 1967, by Harper's Magazine, Inc. Reprinted from the November, 1967 issue of *Harper's Magazine* by permission of the author.

nation for housing, schools, jobs, clean air, and plain civility must be met. But will citizens as well as corporations really profit if these demands are met by private and profit-seeking enterprises? To answer this question, it is well to begin with a slightly cynical analysis of some of the executives' earthy motives.

First of all, it is important to understand that thought is becoming power to a degree beyond the wildest imaginings of a Platonist philosopher-king. Five years ago, Clark Kerr estimated that the production, distribution, and consumption of knowledge already accounted for 29 per cent of the Gross National Product and was growing at twice the rate of the rest of the economy. Last year, the president of IBM declared that the nation was fast approaching a time in which more than half the work force would be involved in processing and applying data. So higher education is no longer the aristocratic province of a tiny upper-class minority.

Second, the executives of the social–industrial complex, and the American people as a whole, have been tutored by militant Negroes, some of whom can't read. Beginning with Martin Luther King's Montgomery bus boycott of 1955, a Negro mass movement rescued America's better self. Eventually, the practical idealism of black men rekindled the spirit of protest on the campus, challenged the churches and the unions, and in effect prepared the country to respond to John Kennedy's summons to action. In the process, social conscience became a political force. Americans suddenly noticed the racial ghettos, the black and white poor, the polluted air, and the squalid facilities of the public sector.

This created, as J. Herbert Hollomon put it on behalf of the Department of Commerce, a "public market." Hollomon urged private industry to go out and build colleges and create new cities. Max Ways of *Fortune* called this approach "creative federalism." It rested, he said, upon "the rapprochement, during the Johnson Administration, between government and business."

Finally, credit must be given to Barry Goldwater for persuading private enterprise to ratify the massive federal activity which the social–industrial complex requires. The ideological unreality of Goldwater's presidential campaign forced businessmen to choose between the risks of the market and the stability of a managed economy. Unhesitatingly, they picked the latter, and in the process endorsed Lyndon Johnson's visionary Great Society.

So the companies have acquired a conscience at that precise moment when, for a variety of technological, social, and political reasons, there is money to be made in doing good.

A great many corporations have already begun to tap the new source of wealth. The knowledge industry now includes among others, General Dynamics, AT&T, General Electric, Time Inc., Philco, Westinghouse, Raytheon, Xerox, CBS, Burroughs Business Machines, and Packard Bell. The city-building industry has attracted Goodyear, General Electric, Humble Oil, Westinghouse, U.S. Gypsum, Sunset International Petroleum, American-Hawaiian Steamship Lines, and even Walt Disney Productions. And this, clearly, is only the beginning of the beginning.

Charles Silberman of *Fortune* was not being extravagant when he wrote recently that the knowledge industrialists, in partnership with the government, are "likely to transform both the organization and content of education, and through it, of American society itself." Clearly such a massive concentration of private power in a traditional public domain is disturbing. I asked one of the top men in the field, Francis Keppel, about it.

How Real Is the Danger?

Keppel, the former United States Commissioner of Education, is now the head of General Learning, a knowledge corporation put together by General Electric and Time Inc. His social conscience long predates the business discovery that thinking is a blue-chip occupation.

There was, Keppel conceded, a danger that business would dominate, rather than serve, American education. Yet, he continued, perhaps the danger has been exaggerated. Of the tens of billions of dollars which America spends each year on schooling, the largest single expenditure is for teachers' salaries. After that, the money goes to construction and maintenance, and only about 4 per cent of the total, or less than $1.5 billion a year, is devoted to instructional materials of all kinds. Therefore, Keppel argued, the giant corporations have not really discovered such a huge market and there really isn't a fiscal motive for "taking over" the system.

Second, Keppel said, decision making in American education is decentralized, authority is vested in a multiplicity of boards, superintendents, and principals. The only way that the knowledge industry can serve a truly public purpose, he believes, is by being clearly subordinate to the educators. The latter must dictate the content of what is to be taught. The corporations can then supply them with services and materials, but they must not impose a curriculum which is designed to satisfy the needs of private profit rather than those of students.

Keppel's second point, it seems to me, involves a crucial distinction. For business can go about solving social problems in either of two antagonistic ways, both of which often employ an identical rhetoric. On the one hand the society can democratically decide what it wants to teach and what kinds of cities it wants to live in. It can then contract out the preparation of materials, the construction work, and even certain advisory functions to the private sector, keeping planning and programming clearly under democratic and political, rather than corporate, control, and making nonprofit institutions the pivot of the whole system. This is what Keppel advocates. On the other hand—here is the sinister potential of the social-industrial complex—America might unwittingly hire business to build a new urban civilization on the basis of the very money-making priorities which brought the old civilization to crisis. The contractor might not simply execute the contract. He might draw it up as well.

Keppel agreed that this second, and ominous, possibility existed. He also conceded that the relative smallness of the educational market might be a cause for pessimism rather than optimism. It could mean that companies would design machines and programs for private use and then, as a careless, money-making afterthought, unload them on school systems as well.

Enthusiastically, even euphorically, the *Wall Street Journal* has reported recent developments which indicate that Keppel's worst fears are already becoming fact. "It is clear," the *Journal* said in one analysis, "both government and industry will play increasingly active parts in deciding what schools will teach and how they will present it." A little later, the paper was more precise: ". . . new schools to a considerable extent have to be built around the electronic gear that will cram them."

This means that fundamental decisions about how learning is to be structured will become part of a corporate struggle for shares of the knowledge market. Each producer will push its own particular educational technology: Xerox, its kind of teaching machines; IBM, computer classrooms; CBS, television; and so on. Obviously, machines, computers, and television may have an enormous contribution to make to American education. But how is one going to decide among them?

Each element in the defense sector—particular industries, branches of the service, "independent" associations for the Army, Air Corps, Navy, and Marines, and even trade unions—has its own special interest (profit for the companies, prestige and power for the officers, jobs for labor). And each one lobbies for strategies which are determined, not by any objective analysis of the needs of the nation, but by its own stake in the decision. The debate over the B-70 bomber during the Kennedy Administration was a classic case in point. A powerful section of the military–industrial complex, led by the Air Force and aiming to serve purposes of its own, mounted a determined campaign against the Administration in favor of proposals which had been rejected by three Secretaries of Defense under Eisenhower and by Secretary McNamara under Kennedy.

Something like this pattern is beginning to emerge within the social–industrial complex. "Business," to quote the *Wall Street Journal* once more, "is turning into an important force for pushing embattled domestic proposals through Congress." An executive of the Department of Housing and Urban Development is quoted as saying, "Each agency has gradually developed a list of firms interested in its field. . . . We know how to turn them on. . . ." At first glance, this might seem to portend a happy situation in which the corporations lend their political power to a public purpose. But, as the experience of the military–industrial complex demonstrates, such procedures lead straight to private alliances between self-interested executives and ambitious bureaucrats. This trend is already quite developed in the cities industry—where, for instance, real-estate men support rent subsidies as a means of attacking public housing—and, as the *Wall Street Journal* realizes, it is going to appear in education too.

A report in the June 17, 1967, *New Republic* vividly illustrates what this might mean. The Office of Education, it said, was considering a grant of $2 million to build a computer classroom for Menominee Indians in Wisconsin. Westinghouse Electric was to develop the hardware which would eventually serve sixty students. This considerable investment would do nothing to help nine hundred other children on the reservation, who are currently receiving inferior education from uncertified teachers, and it is proposed at a time when mechanized teaching is being criticized by some educators as being too impersonal. If *The New Republic* is right, the responsible decision makers had focused not on the needs of the Indian children but on considerations of governmental-corporate *realpolitik*. "The one substantive reason for financing this project," the article held, "is the government's interest in building up the education industry."

As Keppel emphasized, the ultimate outcome of many such apparently alarming trends is still in doubt. The giants in the knowledge industry have been working cautiously with the long run in mind. So far they have been most active in vocational training, both private and public, and the case of the Job Corps may offer some hints of things to come.

Making Schools into Factories

When the Corps was first set up, it was widely hailed as a trail-blazing example of uniting federal idealism and free-enterprise expertise. In general, it has proved a disappointment. Costs have been high (the contracts are, in effect, on a cost-plus basis) and the companies themselves have lost some of their enthusiasm, partly because the escalation of the war in Vietnam makes them feel they can look to McNamara rather than to Shriver for government contracts.

The most relevant perspective of the Job Corps experience is provided by the members and organizers of the American Federation of Teachers. Among the fastest-growing unions in the country, the AFT has consistently fought to improve the quality of education as well as the wages and working conditions of its members. Its somewhat disillusioned view of the privately operated Job Corps camps does not really have to do with money. Rather it centers on the feeling that the companies treated the educators in their employ like so many hired hands, and the schools as if they were factories. John Schmid, the State Federations Coordinator of the AFT, thinks "it is plain that private industry feels that teachers deserve even less of a voice in the formulation of curriculum than do most boards of education." In terms of Keppel's hopes and fears, business is here taking a commanding, autocratic position, not a subordinate one.

Indeed, David Gottlieb, a top analyst in the Office of Economic Opportunity's Plans and Program division, generalized this point in terms of OEO's experience. The conservatives in Congress, he says, are always ready to attack the inadequacies of a federal project run by Harvard, Columbia, or Berkeley, but they're not apt to question the undertaking of a good, down-to-earth businessman. Therefore, Gottlieb argues, the corporate operations are freer from governmental supervision than, say, a Peace Corps training institute directed by a university. And since social programs are always looking for industry and conservative support, there is no great drive to bring these operations under closer public control.

Gottlieb does not think the companies have abused their freedom. Yet the fact that private entrepreneurs in the new knowledge industry already have an immunity from democratic criticism which is denied to nonprofit professors indicates, I believe, a dangerous trend. In the field of education, the exact opposite should hold true.

How Many Million Houses?

But the social–industrial complex is not simply concerned with how Americans think. It may also attempt to decide how the nation lives.

During the hearings chaired by Senator Ribicoff in 1966, the country got some idea of the enormous dimensions of the urban crisis. It is necessary, in President Johnson's phrase, to build a "second America"—between 1966 and 2000, the United States must construct more new housing units than it now possesses. The official estimates call for two million additional units a year, with at least 500,000 of them designed for low-income families. The AFL-CIO says we need 2.5 million new units a year; Walter Reuther's figure is three million. And these things can only be done, businessmen like David Rockefeller told Ribicoff, if there is a federal subsidy to attract the social conscience of profit makers.

This is at least one reason why the backers of the Demonstration Cities (now Model Cities) Act in the fall of 1966 included Rockefeller, Henry Ford, Thomas Gates of Morgan Guaranty Trust, Alfred Perlman of New York Central, and R. Gwin Follis of Standard Oil of California. It also helps explain, I believe, why General Electric is now interested in building a city of 200,000 people from the ground up—using GE products where possible, of course—and why U. S. Gypsum is demonstrating its skill in publicly supported slum rehabilitation and hopes to make an eventual 8 per cent to 10 per cent profit from such work. What was considered "socialism" only yesterday is turning into a sound business investment.

There is a modest precedent for this pattern in the activities of the "civic" executives who appeared in many major American cities in the fifties and sixties. These men were primarily bankers, department-store owners, office-building landlords, and others with a strong business stake in the central city. They mobilized entire communities, used both federal and local funds, and improved the downtown areas to meet the needs of banks, department stores, and office buildings, however, rather than those of the black and white poor.

But the real danger today is not that the social industrialists in the city industry will repeat these mistakes from the past (though some of them will). Nor, with a few exceptions, is the trouble that they are greedy profiteers engaged in some kind of conspiracy against the common good. The issue goes deeper than that. For when business methods are sincerely and honestly applied to urban problems, with very good intention, they still inevitably lead to antisocial results. It is exactly when crass concerns are not paramount that the real problem—the inapplicability of business methods and priorities to the crisis of the cities—emerges most clearly. The testimony of David Rockefeller of Chase Manhattan before the Ribicoff subcommittee is an excellent case in point. Rockefeller is an enlightened, and liberal, banker. Urban problems, he quite rightly told the Senators, "are so closely interrelated they call for the establishment of overall goals and guidance. Public agencies, in most cases, must set the overall goals, then provide assistance and incentives to private enterprise to carry out as much of the program as possible." Senator Charles Percy's original home-ownership plan was most blunt on this point and candid about real motives. His program, he said, "would be attractive to lenders because it promises a *competitive yield and no risk* in addition to its social and philanthropic appeal" [emphasis added].

In theory, the Rockefeller approach subordinates the businessman to the "overall goals" of the community, which are determined by democratic process. But, and in my view this is the crucial point, with all the good will in the world Mr. Rockefeller proposes to interpret those goals according to an economic calculus which can have only antisocial consequences. And since he is talking in terms of five business dollars of investment to every federal dollar (Ribicoff hopes for a ratio of $7 to $1), the fact that he will allocate resources and order his design on the basis of tried, true, and disastrous priorities is of some moment.

"Economic logic," Mr. Rockefeller says, "dictates that the use of real estate be in some meaningful relationship to its value. The projects we have mapped for lower Manhattan are *massive, and generally of a commercial, taxpaying nature*" [emphasis added]. Because this is exactly the approach which contributed much to creating our current problems, it is difficult to see how it will solve them.

In the fifties and sixties, the Rockefeller conception of land use prevailed dramatically in Manhattan. Builders made quite sure that real estate had a meaningful relation to its "value" as narrowly and commercially defined. Huge office buildings were constructed in the center of the city without regard to other possible locations (Harlem, for instance, or Bedford-Stuyvesant) or to alternate use of the resources for abolishing ghettos. An intolerable load thus was placed upon already crowded and grimy transit facilities. And there was, of course, a total lack of concern for history, beauty, and civility.

A task force told Mayor Lindsay in 1966 that "few stores, theaters, or hotels can compete with the arithmetic of office buildings. Those sites which have become legendary, surrounded by character and convenience, often are just the ones the office builders want."

What the cities need are "uneconomic" allocations of resources. Money must be "wasted" on such uncommercial values as racial and class integration, beauty, and privacy. And this is not a simple matter of overall plan either, for it relates to individual trees in front of individual houses as much as to metropolitan areas. Businessmen, even at their most idealistic, are not prepared to act in a systematically unbusinesslike way. And even if they were, they would have no democratic right to do so, for the determinations to be made are in, or should be in, the public domain. In this area, even more than in education, the social industrialists must be subordinated to democratic planning institutions.

Some people, of course, think we can get around the urban crisis by uttering the magic word "rehabilitation." A great many of the social–industrial complex proposals on housing—ranging from HEW's Urban Development Corporation to Senator Percy's homeownership plan—pretend that current problems will be solved if existing slums are refurbished. On this theory, one is absolved from exercising any imagination in creating the second America; all that is necessary is to spruce up the first. The only difficulty with the solution is that it will not work.

To be sure, occasional neighborhoods in big cities can be rehabilitated, thus preserving variety and sometimes even beauty (Georgetown in Washington, D.C., is an ex-slum). But in almost every case this involves removing about three-fourths of the neighborhood's residents, leaving a prettied-up but racially segregated community. Rehabilitation will really work only if it is part of a program to build millions of new housing units for the poor and deprived. In an area like Harlem, for instance, the trouble is not just that people pay exorbitant rents for dilapidated quarters, but also that three, four, and five humans have been crammed into spaces adequate to the needs of single individuals. Both the problem of density and the problem of integration obviously require massive planning at the federal, regional, and local level if they are to be solved. Current federal proposals, however, are necessarily flawed because they count on business to play a dominant role in rescuing cities from the mess which business methods and priorities have created.

Consider, for example, Senator Robert F. Kennedy's anti-slum program. Kennedy has been one of the most conscientious and compassionate of men with regard to the ghettos. He understands that decent housing is utterly central to both the war on poverty and the struggle for civil rights. Yet his $1.5 billion of tax incentives to lure investors into the slums would produce only 400,000 units in seven years, according to the *New York Times*. That is 100,000 fewer units than the *yearly* rate of low-cost housing production advocated by the Council of the 1966 White House Conference on Civil Rights. Moreover, the Kennedy approach might result in breaking a living neighborhood up into a myriad of 100-unit undertakings. The Senator proposes that the federal government insist on minimum standards, but surely they are no substitute for the creative planning of a new urban environment.

And neither is the philosophy expressed by John Notter of the American Hawaiian Land Company, a new-town outfit. "The secret," Notter told *Fortune*, "is speed—getting other people to spend their money instead of you spending yours. Most of our office space is devoted to bookkeepers. In new-town developments that's the real name of the game." And *Fortune* added admiringly, "As American Hawaiian and Humble [Humble Oil] are proving, that's one game large corporations can understand." What kind of a civilization will such a game produce?

If Problem-solvers Take Over

At this point it is possible to synthesize various aspects of the social–industrial complex and to identify a new, and dangerous, American philosophy. It is the ideology of anti-ideology.

The notion that Western society is coming to an "end of ideology" was first articulated by academics, almost all of them liberals, some of them socialists. As Daniel Bell developed the idea, the advanced economies had achieved such material affluence and political consensus that "the old politico-economic radicalism (preoccupied with such matters as the socialization of industry) has lost its meaning. . . ." The result was a "post-industrial" society in which the "new men are the scientists, the mathematicians, the economists, and the engineers of the new computer technology."

This theory was adapted to corporate purpose by business philosophers like Max Ways of *Fortune*. For the proclamation of the end of ideology provided an excellent rationale for the social–industrial complex (Bell and his colleagues had not, of course, intended this use of their thesis). If the public market were still a thirties-like battleground where antagonistic classes and groups fought for dominance, then business, as a minority special interest, could hardly be trusted with the social fate of the majority. But if, as Ways argued, "U. S. politics is making a major turn from the politics of issues to the politics of problems," then all is changed. The old, ideological debate over "issues," in which the radicals proposed to take from the rich and give to the poor, is no more. Problem-solving is the order of the day. And the corporation, as a neutral association of qualified experts, will, for a reasonable fee, promote the public good in an absolutely impartial and scientific way.

The evidence assembled here suggests to me that Ways and the other philosophers of the social–industrial complex are wrong. In producing a knowledge technology, running Job Corps camps, improving the downtown area, proposing priorities for revitalizing entire cities, or suggesting panaceas of slum rehabilitation, the social industrialists are, at every point, pursuing a private interest. And ideology.

What is at stake is nothing less than how the Americans of the twenty-first century are going to think and live. The tragic results of the new and profitable business conscience with which they may have to deal are already foreshadowed in the actual history of one of the first industries to adopt the pretense of unselfishness and anti-ideology: television. .

In the mid-thirties, William Paley of CBS appeared before the Federal Communications Commission. His company, he said, was not primarily a "business organization, except to the extent that economics are a necessary means to social ends. Surely any stress on economics as an end in themselves would betray a lack of understanding of the role which broadcasting plays in every plane of American life." A generation later, after broadcasting had become totally commercialized, Newton Minow described the "wasteland" which had resulted. The Kennedy Administration then exhorted the broadcasters to live up to their social responsibility. In March 1965, after four years of this concentration upon ethics, the FCC reported that hours given to public-service programs had declined by 15 per cent. Walter Lippmann summed up the implications of this particular experience, and his words apply to the social–industrial complex as a whole. "The regulatory method," he wrote, "runs counter to the facts of life. It supposes that broadcasters can function permanently as schizophrenics, one part of the brain intent on profits and another part of that same brain based on public service and the arts."

The knowledge and the cities industries—and the entire social–industrial complex—suffer from this very same schizophrenia, and they are quite capable of making wastelands of the schools and cities. Like CBS in the thirties, they too disdain the "stress of economics" even while they pursue their private interest in the name of anti-ideological public spirit. America, whether it likes it or not, cannot sell its social conscience to the highest corporate bidder. It must build new institutions of democratic planning which can make the uneconomic, commercially wasteful, and humane decisions about education and urban living which this society so desperately needs.

Chapter Three

Locations of Power: Bureaucratic Elites

Our emphasis, to this point, has centered upon the unofficial elites, the private pressure groups which exert influence upon both elected and appointed policy-makers in government. The implication has been that the real formation of public policy takes place outside the public view and that governmental enunciations of policy are simply formalizations for the informal compromises worked out through the cooperation of influential elites.

But almost all federal legislation is actually formulated within the various agencies of the executive branch of government, and we must now inquire into the processes of policy formation within the bureaucratic elites. Increasingly, private interest groups are directing their pressures toward specific agencies in government, instead of lobbying among legislators who do little more than modify agency proposals.

The governmental agencies have found it expedient to take account of private interests early in the policy-formulating process, so as to avoid serious opposition in Congress. In fact, by accommodating many interested parties in the early phase, government agencies are able to amass the support and lobbying skills of the influential elites, and so to increase the chances of their proposals for legislative success.

This chapter's reading selections begin with an article by Betty H. Zisk which traces the course of this process and discusses its relation to democratic ideals.

Formation of Public Policy:
Constitutional Myths
and Political Reality*

Betty H. Zisk

"Power must be finally identified with no one class or group," wrote Pendleton Herring. "It must be handled like a loving cup and passed about lest one of the company grow drunk."[1] Most Americans agree with this statement. Many go still further to assert that it is the power of the *government,* and specifically of the executive, which is most to be feared.

Yet liberties may be lost not only through the *abuse* of power but through *failure to use it* when necessary. Public problems demand rational, long-range solutions. Those whose responsibility it is to make public decisions must frequently move both rapidly and discreetly. One of the ironies of the modern political scene is that the same technological advances which have aided the process of consultation between leaders and the led have also created problems of such magnitude as to make such consultation infrequent and difficult. Individual citizens can follow major congressional debates through their daily newspapers and the radio. They can wire or telephone their national representatives within minutes of the announcement that an important decision is pending. Washington officials, similarly, can be in constant touch with their field offices at home and abroad. This is an era when government fiscal policy can precipitate or help to prevent an economic crisis, when loss of a defense contract can spell disaster for a major metropolitan area, and when a major international crisis has been precipitated by revelation of American

*Betty H. Zisk, "Formation of Public Policy: Constitutional Myths and Political Reality," in *Issues of American Public Policy,* John H. Bunzel, ed., © 1964. Reprinted by permission of Prentice-Hall, Inc., Englewood Cliffs, New Jersey.
[1]*The Politics of Democracy: American Parties in Action* (New York: W. W. Norton & Co., Inc., 1940), p. 46.

espionage activities of which most citizens had been only vaguely aware. Yet extensive public consideration of the most critical problems seems to be impractical. It almost invariably takes place *after* the fact. Lack of detailed information, lack of interest adequate for mastering the intricacies of a complex problem, and the need, on occasion, for policy-makers to act with speed and secrecy combine to divest the citizen of meaningful power over his representatives.

Is there no choice between two unpleasant alternatives—efficient vigorous government by officials remote from public control or fumbling and ineffective policy-making by more democratic means? In short, can responsible government be effective? To discuss the issues raised by this question, it is first necessary to consider in some detail the traditional conception of the democratic policy-making process. It will be argued that classical democratic theory, as presented in most civics texts and implied in political campaign speeches, is more misleading than helpful in describing the democratic political process. It can be considered at best a "first approximation" for a far more intricate reality. After a comparison is drawn between classical theory and current practice, an assessment of the latter will be possible. In the course of such an evaluation, it will also be necessary to examine the key concepts of "responsibility" and "majority rule." It will then be possible to answer the original question—can responsible government be effective?—and its reverse—can effective government be responsible to the majority in a democracy?

Classical Democratic Theory and the Separation of Powers

The authors of the American Constitution established three branches of government. Congress was given "all legislative powers," including the power to levy and collect taxes, to regulate foreign and interstate commerce, to declare war, and to raise and support the armed services. The president, whose most important task was to take "care that the Laws be Faithfully Executed," was authorized to command the Army and Navy, and to make treaties "by and with the Advice and Consent of the Senate." Finally, judicial authority was vested in a system of courts.

But what do these separate investitures of power in the three branches mean? It takes no great leap of the imagination to envisage several possible areas of disputed jurisdiction, particularly between

Congress and the president.[2] Most observers grant the difficulty of drawing a clear line, but traditionally the distinction is stated as follows. Congress has the power to formulate or *make* public policy, spelling that policy out in sufficient detail to guarantee that it is carried out in line with the original formulation.[3] The president and his administration, on the other hand, are entrusted with the task of *carrying out* policies within the limits set forth by Congress. There should be no "administrative discretion," or room for independent judgment and action on the part of the bureaucracy, except on purely routine or insignificant matters. Even in this case, Congress retains not only the right but the *obligation* to correct a situation where it later developed that a "routine" matter carried policy implications.

This division of powers has been justified on the grounds that it protects the individual citizen against the abuse of political authority. In an era when the absolute despotism of European monarchs was only beginning to diminish, the framers of the Constitution wanted, above all, to guard against executive encroachments. At the same time, one lesson of the American experience under the Articles of Confederation had been that a country with a weak central government might perish from lack of adequate direction. Hence the safe course was to establish a set of political institutions with adequate monetary and military powers, yet divide that power in such a way as to limit the authority of any one body. The pattern was completed by reserving residual power for the states and by setting up different methods and timetables for the election or appointment of those who wield national power. In this way, the failure of one constituency to control those to whom it had delegated political power would not necessarily result in the downfall of the whole system.

To Plato's classic question, "Who will guard the Guardians?" this arrangement answered in part, "the other Guardians." Congress,

---

[2]For example, the president as Commander-in-Chief of the Army and Navy can be hampered in carrying out his duties if Congress fails to "support" the armed forces on an adequate level; conversely, congressional power to declare war can be reduced to the level of a rubber stamp if ambassadors act in such a way as to precipitate a crisis, or if the president deploys the armed forces aggressively to the same end.

[3]See Charles S. Hyneman, *Bureaucracy in a Democracy* (New York: Harper & Row, Publishers, 1950), especially Chapter 5, for a classic statement of the necessary dichotomy between policy-making and administration. Hyneman argues that if congressional procedures and organization arrangements are too cumbersome for effective legislative oversight, the solution is not increased executive powers but congressional reform.

jealous of its own prerogatives, would prevent executive abuses, and the courts would watch both Congress and the executive. Congress, really the dominant branch in this conception, would ultimately be responsible to the electorate.

The Place of the Citizen in Policy-Formation

For James Madison, the first public analyst of the Constitution, and for many of the framers, the capacities of the individual voter were far less crucial for the working of the political system than the character and intellectual capacity of those who represent the voters.[4] After the extension of suffrage to all white, natural-born male adults, the emphasis was reversed. The Progressive and Populist reform movements spearheaded the movement to "restore" popular sovereignty. From at least the turn of the century, most democratic theorists have stressed the "watchdog" role of the voter. Thus Woodrow Wilson denounced the congressional committee system and the power of the Speaker of the House primarily because voters were unable to pin the blame for poor laws or administration on any one source, or to redress their grievances through the ballot.[5]

Early advocates of procedural reforms assumed that once institutional barriers were removed, an alert citizenry would be able and eager to control the "irresponsible" legislature and bureaucracy. Thus "dictatorship" by committee chairmen, the power of the Speaker, and the seniority system, which guaranteed that legislators from safe districts held key positions became the chief focuses of attack.

Whether well-informed and politically-involved citizens ever existed in large numbers, even in the much-acclaimed era of the New England town meeting, is a matter of conjecture. Some of the keenest American observers, as exemplified by Walter Lippmann, have long been skeptical on the subject. Lippmann argued, as early as 1936, that most men are capable of making reasonably sensible choices be-

---

[4] Madison believed that elected representatives would "refine and enlarge the public views by passing them through the medium of a chosen body of citizens." Hamilton is quoted by Richard Hofstadter as asserting that the "turbulent and changing" mass of people "seldom judge or determine right." *The American Political Tradition* (New York: Alfred A. Knopf, Inc., 1955), p. 4.

[5] In *Congressional Government: A Study of American Politics* (Boston: Houghton Mifflin Co., 1885).

tween candidates, but little more than this.[6] His views were partially confirmed by the first study in depth of the motives, knowledge, and degree of involvement of individual voters, published in 1944, and by similar studies which have been undertaken more recently.[7] It has been found, for example, that social and economic status, religion, and family preferences are far more important factors in voting choice than are press coverage, speeches by candidates, or arguments over the issues. As the authors of the 1944 study put it:

> The real doubters—the open-minded voters who make a sincere attempt to weigh the issues and the candidates dispassionately for the good of the country as a whole—exist mainly in deferential campaign propaganda, in textbooks on civics, in the movies, and in the minds of some political idealists. In real life they are few indeed.[8]

A realization that the majority of voters is neither well-informed nor intensely interested in politics does not, of course, imply acceptance of the situation as inevitable. One can argue, like Woodrow Wilson, that the institutions of government themselves discourage voter interest, since the voter is unable to hold even those he elects responsible for their actions, much less to control the appointed bureaucracy. Advocates of reform, whether of the internal machinery of Congress,[9] of political parties, or of legislative-administrative relations, usually begin with this premise. Give the people "real" power and they will awaken to their rights and responsibilities. Many civic action groups, like the League of Women Voters, deny

---

[6]See *Public Opinion* (New York: The Macmillan Company, 1936).

[7]Paul F. Lazarsfeld, Bernard Berelson, *et al*, *The People's Choice: How the Voter Makes up His Mind in a Presidential Campaign* (New York: Duell, Sloan & Pearce, 1944). This study was based on a series of intensive interviews with 3,000 voters in Erie County, Ohio, during the 1940 campaign. Later voting studies were undertaken by the same group in New York state, and by the Survey Research Center in Michigan on a nationwide sample of voters. Statistics on voting turnout tell much the same story. In recent years, about 60 per cent of those eligible vote in presidential campaigns, while voting for governors ranges from about 55 per cent in industrial northern states to 22 per cent for most of the South. Primary voting turnout is still lower. See V. O. Key, *American State Politics: An Introduction* (New York: Alfred A. Knopf, Inc., 1956).

[8]Lazarsfeld *et al.*, *op. cit.*, p. 100.

[9]For example, to abolish the seniority rule or to reapportion electoral districts to correct the present overrepresentation of agricultural areas. The latter would not, of course, change the fact that equal representation for all states, regardless of size, in the Senate creates the same effect.

the powerlessness of the voter. They argue that while the interested citizen may not be able to take a prominent part in the specific or technical aspects of the policy-formation process, he *can* make his voice heard on many issues not requiring secrecy or rapid decisions. Senator Jacob Javits of New York, in a pamphlet called "Let Your Congressman Hear From You,"[10] lists several instances of Congressional action base primarily on constituency demonds. Passage of the G.I. Bill of Rights following World War II and defeat of universal military training proposals prior to 1953 are two cases cited. His point is that many congressmen want to follow constituent wishes but cannot do so because of failure of citizens to inform themselves and to make their views known, even in cases where they *could* exercise considerable control over their elected representatives.

Traditional democratic theorists, even while admitting that most voters are relatively uninformed and apathetic, argue that the expression of public views by ordinary citizens is not only a legitimate, but a *necessary* part of the policy-formation process. It should be noted that the relation between legislator and voter is envisioned as a *direct* one. There is no place in the theory for an intermediary such as an interest group, which might both stir up citizen interest and action on the "grass roots" level or act as a spokesman for scores of voters in the corridors of the Senate. Each voter, on the contrary, acts as a unit. He undoubtedly has private economic, social, or religious interests; but his views on public policy are seen as stemming from a sort of personal synthesis, rather than finding expression through separate outlets in the more specialized organizations which might represent him. This image of the voter is consistent with the traditional view of policy formation as a deliberate rather than a bargaining process.

Traditional Views of Interest Groups

There is no reference in the Constitution to those prominent institutions of the modern scene, political parties and pressure groups. In fact, upon consulting James Madison's *Federalist* No. 10, we learn that "factions"—a term which can be interpreted to cover both parties and pressure groups—are potentially dangerous to the country unless their effects are controlled through a representative

---

[10]This pamphlet, privately printed and distributed in about 1950, was written while Javits was still a representative.

system in a large republic.[11] Through this process by which members of any given faction must channel their demands through a representative who also acts as a filter for other factions, the energies which men devote to "selfish" activity can be harnessed for the common good.

Madison's emphasis on the possibility of neutralizing the harmful effects of factions by means of the representative principle is quite different from modern defenses of "the group struggle." Madison envisioned factional activity dispersed through several electoral districts and pressures brought to play upon the individual representative by individuals. He did not foresee the organizational development of both parties and interest groups that has taken place in the past two centuries. Federations of unions, farmers, businessmen, and others now parallel the federal structure of formal government. Similarly, the two parties operate along federal lines. This development means that while a given interest may be dispersed throughout the country, those who share it are able to act with more unity than Madison would have believed possible. The operation of Congress, too, has evolved into something other than a meeting and mutual consultation of semidetached aristocratic statesmen. Many legislators are avowed spokesmen for the predominant interest in their constituency, not simply because they fear defeat at the polls through interest group mobilization of members, but more often because they personally identify with and have been occupationally or otherwise associated with the interest themselves. The development of specialization among legislators and the committee structure of the two houses further this tendency. The labor and education committees are dominated by congressmen from urban constituencies, whereas the agricultural committees reflect rural interests. The relationship between legislators and interest groups is not that of besieged and besiegers—as many advocates of reform, who base their views on the traditional theory outlined here, seem to believe—but rather one of mutual consultation and interaction. Whether this is viewed as constructive cooperation or collusion depends in part on one's conception of the political process.

---

[11]Madison defines a faction as "a number of citizens ... who are united and actuated by some common impulse of passion, or of interest, adverse to the rights of other citizens, or to the permanent and aggregate interests of the community." "The most durable source of factions has been the various and unequal distribution of property."

Traditional Democratic Theory: A Summary

All theories of the process of policy formation in a democracy have certain points in common. They assume that in any society men will differ in their views of the way to utilize material and human resources. These differences will be expressed in the form of competing demands or claims, which are channeled through a body of decision-makers who are recognized as legitimate by the majority. The decisions made by this authoritative body will take the form of laws and administrative arrangements that are binding on the society. As long as most decisions satisfy the people making the original claims, both the institutional arrangements and the choice of men who make and carry out the decisions will be left relatively unchanged. If the majority is dissatisfied, however, a first step will be removal of officeholders from their positions. If dissatisfaction extends to matters of procedures, as might be the case if large numbers of people were excluded from voting, the whole institutional arrangement may be drastically altered through revolution, or through constitutional revision.

In terms of the above set of concepts, the classical theory of the American policy-making process can be summarized as follows: Responsibility for decision making and the carrying out of decisions is vested in two separate authorities, the legislature and the executive. Policy demands on the part of the citizens should be expressed primarily through voting on the basis of issues presented in the campaign, and by means of direct contacts between constituents and representatives. In the event that decisions must be made on complex issues, or on matters on which no well-informed opinion is articulated by the constituency, the legislator will (and should) consult the pertinent sources of information at hand, and be guided by his own conscience. This latter situation will probably occur frequently. If he either ignores his constituents' wishes or makes a decision which they later regard as wrong, they may remove him from office at the next election. The evaluation of demands within the legislature itself is assumed to take place through rational discussion and debate on the merits of policy alternatives, *not* as a bargaining situation conducted on the basis of the relative power of opponents.

According to the classical theory of policy formation, the role of the executive and the bureaucracy is relatively passive, except in the field of foreign policy, where executive leadership has been traditionally recognized as necessary. The executive is expected to advise the legislative decision-makers either in general terms (as in the State of the Union Message) or by providing specific information (as in testimony of Cabinet members before congressional committees), but he may not impose his will upon the legislature. He has no real "claim" to present, except in the realm of foreign policy where he may serve as a spokesman for the national interest. In addition, it is believed that administrative officials should have no part in policy formation. If there appears to be need for administrative discretion in the implementation of policy, the legislature should clarify the original law, since there is no way to hold the administrator responsible to the electorate by threat of removal from office.

Finally, although there is no way to prevent the formation of interest groups without destroying individual liberties, for the most part their existence is deplored. Individuals should present claims to individual legislators; there is no need for, and potentially, a great deal of harm stems from, a "group struggle." This harm arises primarily from the fact that such groups admittedly represent "selfish interests" which *per se* are viewed as contrary to the good of the nation as a whole.

The Intricacies of Reality: An Overview

It is not surprising that the actual political situation in Washington is far more complex than its theoretical outlines. Instead of a straight line of authority extending from individual demands to legislative decisions to the laws themselves, which are then accepted or repudiated by the voters, we have in real life an interweaving and continuing process of action–reaction between claimants and decision-makers.

Who really makes policy? There is no question that the policy-making task is shared by Congress, the Executive, interest groups and others. But a more accurate answer must specify which policy on which occasion. Policy is made by a regulatory commission or an executive bureau, ruling on a tax claim or license application under a broad legislative delegation of authority. It is made by a congressional committee in cooperation with staff members of a few powerful farm organizations, whose prior advice and approval is sought to assure later acceptance by farmers. It can be made by the president and a few close advisors acting in a foreign policy crisis on the basis of a nearly blank check given earlier by Congress.

Who makes policy demands? Again, the answer is not simple.

It may be individual citizens or organized groups. It may be the president speaking on behalf of the nation as a whole, and asking congressmen to forget particular interests and constituency needs, in light of overriding national considerations. It may be the president, or his spokesmen, speaking as the party leader to his fellow partisans in the House of Representatives, pointing out that certain campaign promises must be fulfilled if all of them are to continue in office.

It should be noted, in addition, that policy decisions, once made, themselves become influences on what might be called "the demand environment," in some cases giving birth to new organizations as well as new demands. One instance of this was the creation, by Congress, of the Agricultural Extension Service, which in turn set up local farmers' committees. These committees, originally created to act as channels for government advice and mutual consultation, later joined together as the American Farm Bureau Federation. That organization has since become, as an independent pressure group, the most powerful farmers' group in the country, helping to create policy by the demands it presents.[12]

How are decision-makers held responsible for the laws made? And how are administrative officials, who share in the task of policy formation, prevented from abusing their power? One point which must be kept in mind is that even if election campaigns involved a serious debate of issues, an election at two- or four-year intervals could seldom be interpreted as a clear mandate because of the number of issues involved. Many voters vote for the party whose foreign policy they accept, *in spite of* the domestic stance which is part of the package. Or a voter may like both the foreign policy and civil rights proposals of a party, but find its labor views sheer anathema. Except in a relatively homogeneous constituency, it is almost impossible to ascertain which issues are the crucial ones.

Nor can it be assumed that all candidates will consider themselves bound by a party platform, the most notable example being the civil rights split among the Democrats. Finally, it is not always possible to ascertain the responsible decision-maker, or if it is, to

---

[12]Harry Eckstein, in *Pressure Group Politics: The Case of the British Medical Association* (Stanford, California: Stanford University Press, 1960) presents an excellent theoretical discussion of the influence of official policy on what has here been called "the demand environment," and illustrates it with a study of the British Medical Association, which grew from a small, relatively informal organization to a large and powerful interest group, mainly as a consequence of the National Health Act.

use the ballot to remove him. If the president, with the Senate's approval, appoints ambassadors on the basis of past contributions to the party coffers rather than on the basis of knowledge of the country to which they are being assigned, how will the act of voting solve the problem? If meaningful civil rights legislation or federal aid to education is invariably blocked by a filibuster, or foreign aid appropriations are cut by committee chairmen who are elected by local constituencies on the basis of domestic issues, how can citizens who support these measures use the ballot to change the situation?

The answer to the question "How are decision-makers held responsible?" must be deferred to a later point in this discussion, after a more detailed consideration both of the decision-making process itself and the meaning of the term responsibility. The questions which have already arisen, however, may indicate the complexity of the problem, particularly in contrast to the solutions offered by traditional democratic theory.

The Role of the Executive

If an American statesman of the Federalist era were asked to note the most striking change which has taken place in the policy-formation process, he would be likely to comment on the dominant role of the executive today. It is therefore appropriate to begin at this point. At the outset, three types of executive activity need to be distinguished, of which the third, the initiation and formulation of policy, is the most important. First, there is administrative policy making through daily implementation, interpretation and innovation which arises from previously delegated legal authority. Congress establishes a regulatory commission, which then "makes" policy by the way in which it uses its authority. Second, there is the Executive Agreement, increasingly used in the realm of foreign policy in instances where the need for speed and secrecy as well as the recognition of the intricacies of diplomacy preclude a full Senate debate. Finally, in initiating and working energetically there is considerable executive activity for the passage of specific congressional legislation which the president believes essential for the nation.

There is little question that increasingly complex problems on a *national* scale have created the need for more central direction, more long-range planning, and more rapid solutions than which have been necessary two centuries ago. There is serious question whether Congress, both because of its sheer size and the local constituency basis of support for the legislator, can take the initiative in all aspects of the policy-making process.[13] Students of government have thus placed increasing emphasis on the need for presidential leadership.[14] As David Truman puts it:

> Given the expectations that are focused upon the presidency, the indispensible qualification of a successful White House incumbent is that he be able to lead the Congress. He may need other skills as well but without this ability he can accomplish nothing. He cannot even manage the executive branch unless he can gain from the legislature a minimal acceptance of his leadership.[15]

How does the president carry out this task? If the president and the congressional majority are of the same party, the influence of the White House is considerably stronger than if control is divided. Still, the president cannot rely entirely upon common partisanship. The congressman, after all, depends upon a local constituency with a unique pattern of claims and interests and, in addition, must demonstrate a degree of independence and initiative if he is to continue to receive support. He may even have been elected as a spokesman for a dissident wing of the president's party, as is the case with both the southern Democrats and the more conservative elements in the Republican Party. Although specific political resources are available to him, such as his control over patronage positions in the government, the president's most important weapon is his symbolic status and reputation as a leader who is at most times "above party," who speaks for the nation as a whole and who can thus appeal for public support over the heads of congressmen. In recent years, the important presidential decisions involving foreign and military policy have contributed to his strengthened position because it is the chief executive who deals with other heads of state and has access to the latest and most accurate information.

---

[13]The problem which arises from the local nature of the congressman's support is that he often feels that he must look after constituency needs first, if he is to be re-elected. Thus, he may be compelled to work for farm price supports, tariffs protecting inefficient textile mills, or segregated schooling—if this is what his constituents demand—in spite of his realization that such local "benefits" may not be in accord with the imperatives of national policy.

[14]Although some argue instead for "responsible party government" modeled on the British system.

[15]David Truman, *The Governmental Process* (New York: Alfred A. Knopf, Inc., 1951), p. 402.

The president's power is limited, however, because he often cannot ask for help from congressional leaders without granting in return concessions that may ultimately compromise his own position. Thus, he may have to promise southern Democrats that he will postpone efforts on civil rights in return for their support of retraining programs for the unemployed. He also is aware that if he makes too many bargains of this sort, he risks losing most of his objectives. In addition, in working with a narrow majority of administration supporters, he may need to use mildly coercive methods on a few men, such as the threat of fewer patronage positions for their constituents, or refusal to campaign for them in the next election. Again, overuse of such techniques may create hostility which will plague him in the future. Thus the president must take care to "guard his power stakes."[16] He must choose the issues for which he will make an all-out effort with care and discretion to avoid showdowns on issues where he cannot win, unless such showdowns are precipitated with the intention of taking the issue to the voters as part of an educational campaign. He is unwise to do this except on extraordinary occasions, particularly if he wants further cooperation from Congress. In short, he must protect both his political reputation and his bargaining position. In a period where foreign policy crises are recurrent, he may want to reserve most of the leverage he has for this field. On the other hand, he may believe that new sources of electoral strength and congressional support can be gained through a strong drive on domestic problems. A president who knows and enjoys the use of power must possess something approaching a sixth sense in deciding when and how to use it to further what he believes is in the nation's interest.

Congress and "The Group Struggle"

The policy-making process is sometimes referred to as "the group struggle." Although traditional theorists have usually viewed decision-making institutions as deliberative bodies presumably reaching agreement on the basis of a "national interest" a more appropriate analogy might be that of *bargaining*. The goals of competing claimants are met in proportion to the power of the

---

[16]Richard E. Neustadt, *Presidential Power: The Politics of Leadership* (New York: John Wiley & Sons, 1960), upon whose analysis much of this section is based, is the author of this phrase.

opponents on a given issue. Power in political bargaining may depend on a number of factors—financial resources, prestige, the number of people the claimant purports to represent, tactical skills, the position that he holds—in short, anything which can be used to induce others to behave in the way one desires. A senator may be powerful not only because of the position he occupies but because he gets along with his colleagues, has a grasp of technical details in a few fields, and maintains good relations with outside groups, voters, and the press. An interest group may be powerful because of the size of its membership, its key role in the national economy, its ability to "get the ear" of the president, its skill in presenting valuable information to legislators, its ability to arouse its members, and, not least of all, its financial resources.

While the formal history of a given Senate bill may be a relatively simple one—introduction, followed by referral to the relevant committee, public hearings, debate, and then passage or defeat—the informal history is often more interesting and complex. A bill may have been born at a luncheon of interest group representatives, one of whom later went to "sound out" a senator he knew well. The next stage might be a strategy meeting in the senator's office, with several legislative assistants of other senators present plus the original interest group spokesmen. A timetable is set up, various group representatives are asked to contact the senators they know best, while others agree to send out information bulletins and calls for help to their local offices throughout the country. One of the senator's assistants may be assigned the job of serving as the center for an informal network of "private" and "public" personnel for as long as the issue is alive.

Frequently a bill originates with a senator, whose first step may be to call in these same group representatives, remind them of past favors, and ask for their help on this new project. Perhaps the cooperation begins at a later point, when word is passed along that more witnesses are needed at the committee hearings. Since 90 per cent of the bills passed by Congress are approved in substantially the same form that the committee "reports" them and since the vast majority of bills introduced in Congress die in committee without ever reaching the floor, the committee usually becomes the focus of attention, whether or not public hearings are actually held.

Many congressmen are themselves members of interest groups, notably the National Rivers and Harbors Congress, the American Legion, the American Bar Association, and several farm organizations. Even those who are not formally affiliated with a group are products of their own past experience and beliefs and may identify with the most prominent interests of their constituencies on an almost unconscious level. Congressmen and Washington representatives of interest groups frequently work together on a long-term basis, rendering mutual assistance as needed. Thus a senator may receive help on an issue of minor concern to a given group because that group expects in turn to ask the senator's help on a different issue. It is not unusual for senators, representatives and interest group representatives to plan and work together on an issue of mutual interest over a period of years. Many interest groups cooperate with each other on a continuing basis through informal clearing houses and action groups in such policy areas as foreign trade, foreign aid and technical assistance appropriations, civil rights, and civil liberties. The same spokesmen for farmers, businessmen, and labor, who a few weeks earlier may have been bitter opponents on a domestic issue, appear to be able to close ranks in order to further mutual goals.

In a major congressional debate issues are ultimately decided by the relative strength of two or more loosely aligned opposing blocs of "private" and "public" individuals and organizations. For example, in the "tidelands oil" controversy which reached its peak in 1953, the advocates of state control over the oil resources of the tidelands"[17] included the major oil companies; the National Association of Attorneys-General; the Departments of Justice, Interior, and State; the President; most of the newspapers in the country; the Senate Majority Leader; and key members of the Senate and House Interior and Insular Affairs Committees. The proponents of federal title to the resources in question included representatives of farm, labor, educational and religious organizations, officials from the previous Democratic administration, the so-called elite press, and a group of eighteen senators, mostly from the Northeast and West. This controversy, which began in 1937, had given rise to three Supreme Court decisions and two presidential vetoes. It had also figured prominently in the 1952 presidential campaign. Feeling ran so high that senators who were normally outspoken opponents of

---

[17]The correct term is the "marginal sea." The true tidelands, or land covered and uncovered by the ebb and flow of the tide, were not at issue. The land subject to controversy lay between the outer edge of the tidelands and the three-mile limit. In addition, the farther ring of land between the marginal sea and the Outer Continental Shelf entered into the debate at a later point and a later Supreme Court decision.

the "filibuster" when used in debates on civil rights delayed the Senate for three weeks in an effort to "educate the public" on the nature of this "giveaway of national resources," culminating in Senator Wayne Morse's record-breaking speech of 22 hours and 26 minutes. Their opponents felt, with equal conviction, that basic and "sacred" states' rights were involved. Yet the issue was decided in favor of the advocates of state control, not primarily on its merits but on the basis of the power of the two groups. As long as those who favored federal title included in their number not only the Supreme Court but the President, they were able to hold out against the majority of both houses at Congress. However, after a candidate who was sympathetic to the forces of state control was elected to the presidency in 1952, the battle was lost.

Although the shift of power from one side of a controversy to another is not always so striking, the underlying dynamics are similar. It is for this reason that interest groups and legislators alike work feverishly to gain as many allies as possible in the early stages of a struggle, and why working relationships are actively maintained between the official and unofficial policy-makers over a period of years. The lone individual who writes to his congressman after reading of a debate in progress is usually several weeks or months too late; the lines have already been drawn and the decision all but foreclosed on the basis of the strength of the opponents. This is not to imply that the merits of the arguments on both sides of an issue are irrelevant—rather, that they are only one of many factors in the struggle.

The Modern Citizen: Membership, Protest and the Vote

The single most important avenue of expression open to the citizen is, in the light of the foregoing considerations, his affiliation with an interest group. This is because the interest group has been "co-opted" into the policy-making process itself. Thus the line between "public" and "private" organizations is blurred, and the citizen, through his interest group affiliations, becomes a part of the public process.

It should not be assumed, however, that political acts of unaffiliated individuals are always futile. The tradition of individual action and protest is an honored one, and still bears fruit. Men continue to register their views on public policy through letters, telegrams and personal contacts with public officials, and to receive answers, if not agreement, from their representatives. The effectiveness of this approach will, of course, vary with the issue, the citizen, and the legislator. A letter from Albert Einstein, Henry Ford, or the chairman of a state party organization would undoubtedly carry more weight than those from less prominent people. Obviously, some congressmen treat mail from constituents more seriously than did a Pennsylvania Representative who answered a letter opposing the proposed Bricker Amendment to the Constitution with the statement that despite overwhelming constituent pressure against that proposal, he would support it because he was in a far better position to understand it. Most legislators, however, arrange to have their staffs keep a rough count of mail pro and con on an important issue— and they personally read occasional pieces of mail which seem to be uniquely informative, "typical," or from an extremely important source.

What, finally, is the function of voting? In spite of the shortcomings of the ballot as a means of insuring specific action on given policies, it should not be concluded that the vote is meaningless. Within the context of interparty consensus on the broad lines of some policy issues, there is nonetheless room for considerable difference of opinion within what might be termed the middle range of alternatives. For example, in the field of foreign policy, both major parties are committed to an internationalist and militarily defensive stance. This commitment means that neither the pacifist nor the isolationist is given a serious hearing. Yet those who wish to argue the relative merits of differing defense strategies (for example, massive retaliation versus graduated deterrence) or differing organizational arrangements (emphasis on technical assistance through the United States, the State Department, or within a regional group) will command attention. And it is within this middle range that most arguments over issues, particularly during election campaigns, take place.

The radical voter, that is, the man who stands outside of the middle range placing the emphasis on the morally correct rather than the possible, will not have a "real" choice between candidates. He will, perhaps, be able to take comfort in the fact that his protest vote, in combination with others, may lead to later adoption of part of his party's platform by the major parties.[18] The moderate, in

---

[18]Murray S. Stedman and Susan W. Stedman, *Discontent at the Polls* (New York: Columbia University Press, 1950) point out that farmer–labor parties, if judged not by success in electing candidates but in terms of policies advocated, have over a period of years gained most of their goals as a result of this process. Civil service reform is one of the many issues cited as a minor party plank later taken over by the major parties and written into law.

contrast, can usually find important differences between the parties, particularly on domestic issues like government regulation of business and labor, or social welfare measures.

The act of voting should not be viewed as a specific mandate. Later events may preclude the proposed action. The legislator or perhaps the president may feel it prudent and necessary to compromise on some points to achieve other objectives. Nor is there any necessity for accepting as an absolute the idea that a congressman is little more than a cash register, dutifully ringing up his constituents' wishes as expressed. Edmund Burke in 1774 presented the classic argument for the concept of legislator as a trustee who relied primarily on his own knowledge and judgment of the situation. A great many American voters apparently agree with Burke's stand insofar as they admittedly vote more on the basis of candidate personality and their own long-range party loyalties than on the merits of the specific issues of the campaign.

Some elections, however, have reflected a more dramatic reversal of public opinion than the foregoing discussion might imply. The ability of the president and Congress to act upon such a change in voter attitudes has varied in accordance with the limitations discussed, and with the strength of the working majority. Even when a shift in opinion occurs between presidential elections, however, the result is not always stalemate. The Republican Congress elected in 1946 produced a large number of laws, including the Taft-Hartley Act, in accordance with an apparent rejection by the electorate of part of the earlier philosophy of the New Deal, in spite of the continuation of a Democratic president in the White House. A more recent example of a change in public opinion that was later reflected in public policy was the opposition to federal control of natural resources that developed at the time of the 1952 presidential election.

Conclusion: Responsibility and Majority Rule

The process of policy formation in the United States consists of a continuous interplay between claimants and decision-makers, both of whom concern themselves with the allocation of the country's human and natural resources. Members of Congress, the president, administrative officials, the political parties, and interest groups share the task of policy formation, alternating between the pressing of policy demands and the evaluation of others. It has been noted how this process differs in several major respects from the picture presented by traditional democratic theory. Democratic theorists in the United States have stressed the supremacy of a legislature responsible to the independent voter. Yet the policy-making task as it exists today is shared by many individuals and institutions not directly responsible to the voter. It is necessary, therefore, to return to some of the questions raised at the beginning of this discussion. Can it be said that policy is shaped by men who are in any sense responsible to the will of the majority? The answer depends on the definition of two key terms, "responsible" and "majority."[19] In the classical conception, responsibility meant accountability to some outside body or group of individuals for one's actions. The philosophy of majority rule was taken to mean the right of one half plus one of the voters to decide any issue under any circumstances, either directly or through the right to influence and remove representatives. In this sense, responsibility and majority rule do not exist in the United States. In fact, it may be argued that unlimited majority rule has never existed under our Constitution since there are certain issues—for example, the provisions of the Constitution itself—where more than a bare majority is required for change.

If, however, it is recognized that (1) the term "responsibility" has a second meaning—that of *rationality*—which at times may impose limits on the responsiveness of decision-makers to the majority, and (2) the term "majority" itself contains some ambiguities (does it mean simply one-half plus one of those who feel strongly enough to vote? or is there some way in which the concept can be redefined to take into account *intensity* of opinions?), then it may be that the classical view of the prerequisites for democracy is inadequate.[20] It may be necessary to ask a different set of questions about the policy-making process.

There remain two problems which deserve brief mention. The first is whether most American citizens have access to the informa-

---

[19]The analysis in this section follows the line of reasoning put forth by J. Roland Pennock, "Responsiveness, Responsibility and Majority Rule," *American Political Science Review* (September, 1952), 790–807; and Robert Dahl in *A Preface to Democratic Theory* (Chicago: University of Chicago Press, 1956), and *Who Governs?* (New Haven: Yale University Press, 1961), especially in Book VI.

[20]Pennock, *op. cit.*, points out that the concept of responsibility doesn't take into account possible conflicts in the *consequences* of public demands—conflicts of which the public itself may not be aware. Public desire for "free trade," implying no tariffs, quotas, etc. which interfere with the free movement of commodities may conflict with public conceptions of national defense imperatives, for example, the desire to subsidize economically inefficient domestic industries in order to preserve skills needed for war limitations imposed on imports from hostile nations. (Example is this author's, not Pennock's.) ...

tion needed for formulation of their own policy preferences. Do they, at the same time, have the means for expressing these preferences in as much detail as they would like in such a way that, at least over a period of time, these preferences will be acted upon? Second, is there any way to guarantee that those who are given the task of making and carrying out policy actually *do so* in general accord with citizen policy preferences? It is important to note that what is involved here is not only the idea that decisions should *not* be taken against clearly expressed public policy preferences, but that decisions *should* be made and actions *should* be taken to carry out these decisions. In other words, failure to act at all is as undesirable as taking action against the wishes of the majority of the people.

It has already been seen that the majority of voters do not possess the interest and information assumed by classical democratic theory, and that even if they did it would be difficult for them to impose sanctions on policy-makers. This does not mean, however, that they are totally without influence. Over a long period of time most Americans maintain a relatively stable set of values ("the democratic creed") with which they believe American political institutions are consistent. The area of disagreement arises over particular *means* taken to put their beliefs into action when dealing with specific problems. Many citizens disagree at times with the means chosen by policy-makers, but because of lack of interest, information and skill in reaching the policy-makers, they take little action on the basis of this disagreement. There is, however, a relatively small group of people who make up what Robert Dahl calls "the political stratum,"[21] those who *are* more skilled, interested, and informed and who have more contact with professional politicians. If members of this stratum disapprove of policy decisions, they attempt to influence the policy-makers through the press, political parties, and interest groups. They can present demands on issues not previously dealt with by policy-makers and use their influence to limit or reverse policies already made. This process of checks and reversals also involves the nonpolitical majority to the extent that it contributes to or joins in the formation and actions of interest groups and parties through which the politically active work. It is only when a large number of the politically active become dissatisfied with the way in which the formal policy-making body works, how-

---

[21]Dahl, *Who Governs?* This group of citizens is roughly equivalent to what Walter Lippmann, *op. cit.,* calls "the attentive public."

ever, that the majority of the people become intensely involved. At this point both the professional policy-makers and the political stratum appeal to the public for help in settling the dispute.

Thus it appears that the political beliefs of the majority are relevant in that occasional appeals to "the people" are made and are framed in terms of their beliefs.[22] But it can also be seen that the process of policy making does not conform to the principle of "majority rule" in the classical sense. Rather, it is a rule by minorities who depend for their continued influence upon a relatively stable consensus among the public at large. Responsibility of decision-makers is maintained by an indirect process. Leaders of interest groups and parties must adhere, at least on a minimal basis, to their members' beliefs if they are to continue to wield influence. Administrators must adhere to professional standards and must be able to anticipate public needs to carry on their daily task of interpretation and facilitation.[23] The president must maintain his professional reputation by judicious use of his power. Both the president and members of Congress must face elections. An even more important check on their actions, however, may be the sanctions imposed by fellow policy-makers. A senator or president who operates within the limits set by the political community can be more effective than one who ignores those limits.[24]

If this system of "policy making by minorities" is evaluated and judged by comparing it to the New England town meeting ideal

---

[22]Dahl, *Who Governs? op. cit.*, points out that professional politicians also share these beliefs, and he hypothesizes that the internalization of values shared by the public and decision-makers alike is probably a far more effective "check" or guarantee of responsibility than formal institutional arrangements can be.

[23]Carl Friederich, in "Public Policy and the Nature of Administrative Responsibility," *Public Policy, 1940* (Harvard Yearbook of the Graduate School of Public Administration, Friedrich and Masons, eds.) argues that the administrator's need to justify his actions before professional colleagues ("the fellowship of science"), in combination with his anticipation of public needs, is far more effective in maintaining administrative responsibility than fear of sanctions by the legislature. Herman Finer, in "Administrative Responsibility in Democratic Government," *Public Administration Review* (Summer, 1941), 335–50, takes issue with this viewpoint.

[24]See Donald R. Matthews, *U.S. Senators and Their World* (Chapel Hill: University of North Carolina Press, 1960) for an elaboration of this point. Matthews argues that senators who adhere to informal "rules of the game" generally accepted by other senators, are far more effective in achieving their goals than those who ignore these rules. Similarly, the senator who becomes expert in one or two specialized fields is heeded and respected more than a generalist.

of direct democracy, it will be found seriously wanting. If, on the other hand, it is judged in terms of the nature of the public problems which must be solved, there is less cause for concern. The number of demands, and the complexity of the means that must be utilized to reconcile and fulfill them, would stagger the imagination of a John Adams or a James Madison. There is further reassurance in the fact that the political minorities who exercise power can only continue to do so if the majority is satisfied. Individual political apathy and ignorance should not be viewed with resignation or complacence. Nonetheless, those who work for enlarged public participation must be warned neither to despair nor to set their sights on unattainable goals.

The Administrative Revolution*

Bertram Gross

In the article that opens this book, Edward Shils emphasized the positive aspects of the mass society. Bertram Gross, an expert in organizational theory, maintains that the mass society has become an organizational society, and that the effect of such a bureaucratic culture is to increase the dehumanization and alienation of member individuals. In Gross' mass society the individual's ability to influence his government is thwarted by a monolithic bureaucracy which formulates rules largely in response to pressures from private elites.

In the early days of the Industrial Revolution there arose a vigorous literature of protest against the degradation of labor in filthy factories and sweatshops and of life in teeming urban slums. In the more advanced societies of the world these horrors have considerably diminished. There is reason to expect they may be eliminated. The leaders of developing nations often believe they can partially skip this stage, or at least ameliorate conditions through welfare services.

But the literature of revolt was never limited to physical conditions. It also accused large-scale organizations of committing the following "crimes" against the individual:

---

*Reprinted with the permission of The Macmillan Company from *The Managing of Organizations: the Administrative Struggle*, by Bertram M. Gross. Copyright © by The Free Press of Glencoe, a Division of The Macmillan Company, 1964.

—treating him like a cog in a machine
—subordinating him to the organization
—alienating him from truly human relations with others, and
—promoting mental breakdown.

While the other charges have become weaker, these have become stronger. They are heard both in developed and developing economies. They have swelled into a formidable literature of revolt against organizations, bureaucrats and administrators.

Little research has yet been undertaken to provide the evidence backing up these charges, let alone help formulate them more precisely. Thus most of the literature in which they are contained is really "literature." It is penned mainly by reformers, satirists, commentators and artists, although some of them may don the robes of sociologist, psychiatrist, or economist.

Much of this indictment is excellent literature. It seems to ring true. It depicts an important aspect of life in the modern world, even though the colors may sometimes seem unduly somber. It reflects widespread fears and anxieties, themselves a part of life in the administered society. It raises questions that demand attention.

The "Fractionation" of Work

As far back as in the days of Adam Smith, economists noted that with the growing division of labor the worker's "dexterity at his own particular trade seems in this manner to be acquired at the expense of his intellectual, social and marital virtues."[1] Karl Marx observed that the system of concentrating individual work upon minute parts of a total production process

> converts the laborer into a crippled monstrosity, by forcing his detailed dexterity at the expense of a world of productive capabilities and instincts; just as in the States of La Plata they butcher a whole beast for the sake of his hide or tallow. Not only is the detail work distributed to different individuals, but the individual himself is made the automatic motor of a fractional operation...[2]

The monotony of fractionated work has also tended to remove the worker from creative participation in the work process. But as [Peter] Drucker has pointed out the problem of monotony is minor; in many circumstances, in fact, monotony has its virtues. The more

---

[1]Adam Smith, *The Wealth of Nations* (New York: Modern Library, 1937), p. 735.

[2]Karl Marx, *Capital* (New York: Modern Library, 1936), p. 396.

serious problem is that "the worker has not enough relation to his work to find satisfaction in it. He does not produce a product. Often he has no idea what he is doing or why. There is no meaning in his work, only a pay check."[3]

[Robert] Merton has carried this thought further in his observation that "the splintering of work tasks involves *loss of public identity of the job*." Can one's wife, children or friends find any social meaning, any claim to respect or deference in one's work in turning three screws, watching four gauges or aligning five parts of a part of a part? This absence of social meaning goes further toward alienating the worker from his job and in making his wage his chief symbol of social status.[4]

With only minor adaptations this analysis applies as much to the white collar worker, technician and manager himself as to the manual worker. The clerk may have even less contact than the worker with the goods or services which are produced; he deals with paperwork and routines. The technician immerses himself in the labyrinth of technique; he too often tends to become an example of what [Thorstein] Veblen called "trained incapacity." The manager occupies himself more and more with the production of power, prestige, profits and relations with people; he has less and less to do with the goods or services which his organization produces.

The effect on personality is particularly striking in the professional world. Here the division of intellectual labor has led to an unbelievable degree of specialization and subspecialization. The deeper the professional man burrows into his specialty, the greater the social distance which is created between himself and his fellows, including other professionals. On the credit side, this may serve as a tight little island of emotional security, protected against all intruders by a Maginot line of impenetrable jargon. On the debit side, this often also insulates him from creative contact with the real problems of real life, which usually defy neat classification in terms of disciplines and subdisciplines.

Subordination to the Organization

As an abstract proposition, one might assume that a person working in a narrowly specialized area could both apply his creative spirit

---

[3]Peter F. Drucker, *The Concept of the Corporation* (New York: John Day Co., 1946), p. 158.

[4]Robert K. Merton, *Social Theory and Social Structure* (Rev. ed.; New York: The Free Press of Glencoe, 1957), p. 139.

within this area and function as an independent individual outside it. However, a growing body of social criticism suggests that with many or even most people exactly the opposite may be the case. Albert Schweitzer is only one of many who have claimed that "overorganized societies" have "shattered" the human spirit.[5] David Reisman and his associates[6] maintain that the typical "character type" in the modern world has become the "other-directed person." This type has a "built-in radar set" which gives him continuous messages on what is expected of him. Although he enjoys a higher standard of living than his predecessors, he pays for this improvement by having to live in "a centralized and bureaucratized society and a world shrunken and agitated by the contact—accelerated by industrialization—of races, nations and cultures." His main concern is not with action but with relations with other people. He manipulates them or is manipulated by them. He becomes the victim of "false personalization" or "enforced privatization." The messages from his radar set tend to dominate his life.[7]

The same basic idea has been further developed by those who have written about the "mass man" and the "organization man." According to Lewis Mumford, the human being produced by modern civilization tends to become

> . . . a mass man: incapable of choice, incapable of spontaneous, self-directed activities: at best, patient, docile, disciplined to monotonous work to an almost pathetic degree, but increasingly irresponsible as his choices become fewer and fewer: finally, a creature governed by his conditioned reflexes—the ideal type desired, if never quite achieved, by the advertising agency and the sales organizations of modern business or by the propaganda office and the planning bureaus of totalitarian and quasi-totalitarian governments.[8]

In 1959 a general of the U.S. Strategic Air Command issued "a directive dividing each squadron into groups of three to five men

---

[5]Victor Gollancz, *Man and God* (Boston: Houghton Mifflin Co., 1951), p. 216.

[6]David Riesman, Nathan Glazer, and Reuel Denny, *The Lonely Crowd* (New Haven: Yale University Press, 1951).

[7]The "other-directed" person is contrasted with "the tradition-directed personality," who is to a large extent influenced by the culture of his society as transmitted to him by the small number of individuals with whom he comes into contact, and the "inner-directed personality," who has inside of him a "psychological gyroscope" of his own.

[8]Lewis Mumford, *The Conduct of Life* (New York: Harcourt, Brace & World, 1951), p. 14.

and assigning a non-commissioned officer to find out just what 'the airman does with his off-duty time, whom he associates with and to counsel him in the areas where he shows a weakness.' Everything from the airman's automobile to the cut of his hair was to be looked into." When the directive was publicly criticized, the Air Force quickly withdrew it. The general who had issued it ruefully described the system as "only what any father would be doing for his son." In commenting upon the rescinded order, an editorial in the *New York Times* (December 17, 1959) hinted that the new order may have done little more than describe more vividly a policy that had been in force for some time. But neither the general nor the editorial writer pointed out that the "big brother" or "big father" approach was not the invention of the Air Force. The generals merely borrowed it from large corporations which have long followed the practice of keeping close track of the private lives of administrative personnel. In these organizations personal advancement—once one gets past the barrier of initial appointment—is often made conditional upon the type of person one marries, his use of leisure time, the kind of friends he associates with, and a host of other personal characteristics having no direct relationship with the job he is supposed to perform.

The tyranny of the organization has also served as a theme used by modern artists in surrealist painting, in music, in poetry and in the dance. Its most vivid development, however, is found in the novel. In the early 1930's Aldous Huxley wrote his well-known *Brave New World,* a projection into a future six or seven hundred years away. This was a world in which individualism was destroyed by the "nightmare of total organization." A little less than twenty years later, after the world had a chance to view the works of both Nazism and Stalinism, George Orwell published his *1984.* The difference between the two worlds is that for Huxley individualism was eradicated by a scientific caste system and the abolition of free-will through methodical conditioning and the use of drugs and various hypnotic techniques. Orwell's dictators achieve the same objectives through terror and espionage. Looking back upon his prophecies from the vantage point of 1958, Huxley concludes in *Brave New World Revisited* that they "are coming true much sooner than I thought they would" and that both democratic and communist regimes are moving toward a society organized along Huxley or Orwell principles.

A picture of modern society which is in many ways even more terrifying is presented in the strange and nightmarish novels of the Czechoslovakian writer, Franz Kafka. In *The Castle* K. wanders aimlessly in the lower levels of a labyrinthine bureaucracy peopled by strange faceless creatures whose private lives are dominated by their own conceptions of the anonymous occupants of the unseen, unvisited Castle. *The Trial* recounts the experiences of another K. who is arrested on charges that are never specified. Even on the last pages, when a knife is finally plunged into K.'s aching heart, the reader still does not know the identity or the motives of those who have dominated, and finally ended, K.'s life.

A softer, but still rather devastating, picture is painted by William H. Whyte in his analysis of the person who not only *works* for The Organization but who *belongs* to it as well. This is "The Organization Man." While he may give occasional lip-service to the Protestant Ethic of individualism and risk-taking, his life is conducted for him by the new Social Ethic which glorifies the virtues of belongingness, togetherness, conformity and adjustment to the group. "The Corporation Man is the most conspicuous example. But he is only one, for the collectivization so visible in the corporation, has affected almost every field or work." The seminary student, the doctor, the physics Ph.D., the research intellectual, the young engineer and the young lawyer—they are all being molded into organization men who find a refuge from the harsh uncertainties of freedom within the bosom of the organization and who soon become past masters at the great art of "playing it safe." If an organization man should try to resist, if he should reassert some measure of his own individuality, he faces a dilemma. "It is not a case of whether he should fight against black tyranny or blaze new trails against patent stupidity. That would be easy—intellectually, at least! The real issue is far more subtle. For it is not the evils of organization life that puzzle him, but *its very beneficence*. He is imprisoned in brotherhood."[9] It might be added that there are still stronger bonds than beneficence and brotherhood. Many individuals throw themselves completely into their organizational work. For the organization, which serves for them as a symbol and substitute for mother, wife and self, they are willing to sacrifice family relations, friendships, leisure, personal development and individuality itself. It is no exaggeration to say that they "love that organization." In place of the light ardors of adolescence and early marriage they are consumed by passionate dedication to an organization which swallows them up in its all-enveloping embrace.

---

[9]William H. Whyte, Jr., *The Organization Man* (New York: Simon and Schuster, 1956), p. 12.

Social- and Self-Alienation

With the growth of closer relations between the individual and the group, one might think that the result would be closer relationships between people. Critics of the administrative society grant the new closeness but strongly maintain that these relationships are becoming increasingly nonhuman.

"Due to the bigness of the apparatus to be administered, and the resulting abstractification," observes [Erich] Fromm,

> the bureaucrats consider neither with love nor with hate, but completely impersonally; the manager–bureaucrat must not feel, as far as his professional activity is concerned; he just manipulates people as though they were figures or things. . . . Everybody is to everybody else a commodity, always to be treated with a certain friendliness, because even if he is not of use now, he may be later.[10]

Fromm calls this alienation.

Still more serious is the tendency toward man's alienation from himself.

> The alienated person is out of touch with himself as he is out of touch with any other person. . . . His sense of self does not stem from his activity as a loving and thinking individual but from his socio-economic role. . . . He experiences himself, not as a man, with love, fear convictions, doubts, but as an abstraction, alienated from his real nature, which fulfills a certain function in the social system.[11]

Or else as a thin substitute for a deeper sense of self, he plays a series of roles in relation to others, roles which have the function of winning friends and gaining approval.[12]

A parallel tendency is found in the trend toward the dehumanization of cultural values. Entertainment becomes a highly organized mass activity which emphasizes escapism. Education becomes preoccupied with techniques and utilities. The humanities decline as a

---

[10]Erich Fromm, *The Sane Society* (New York: Holt, Rinehart and Winston, 1955), pp. 136, 139.

[11]In this sense the meaning of "alienation" is close to that assigned it in the nineteenth century when it was regarded as a form of self-estrangement just a little less serious than insanity. This meaning is still preserved in the use of "alienist" to refer to a doctor who deals with the insane.

[12]Erich Fromm, *op. cit.*, pp. 120–122, 142–143.

field for study and development. Intellectualism becomes suspect. The materialistic values of wealth, efficiency and status become dominant. The academic pedant who teaches Shakespearean drama within the confines of textual exegesis, and thus misses contact with one of the great adventures of the human spirit, also contributes to the dehumanizing process. The fact that he may be a stalwart defender of the humanities against the natural sciences, the professions and such new intruders as business and public administration is merely a pathetic example of the ease with which, in a materialistic society, the forms of humanism may be honored by those who destroy its substance.

Frustration and Neurosis

Anyone with a modicum of organizational experience knows how easily organizational life can lead to frustration and how numerous are the opportunities it provides for the venting of aggression upon others. [Chris] Argyris[13] has summarized a vast amount of research which gives depth and meaning to this common-sense observation. In fact, he has formulated the thesis that formal organization itself requires "behavior that tends to frustrate, place in conflict, and create failure for psychologically healthy individuals." In part, the result may be a variety of defense reactions (such as daydreaming, aggression, ambivalence, regression, projection), apathy and disinterest toward the organization, and the creation of informal groups to sanction the defense reactions, apathy and disinterest. Another result may be a further stimulus to climb the organizational ladder and reach heights where individual goals are presumably less in conflict with those of the organization. Unfortunately, most of the research work which Argyris draws upon to substantiate his hypothesis deals with people at the lower levels of the bureaucratic hierachy. Insufficient attention is thus given to the innumerable factors making for frustration and "management ulcers" at the higher levels of the bureaucracy and among the top executives and members of the directorates.

Organizational life at all levels provides abundant opportunity for people to solve their internal conflicts through such neurotic solutions as hostility and aggression, fixation and compulsiveness, compliance and helplessness, withdrawal and isolation, sublimation and displace-

---

[13]Chris Argyris, *Personality and Organization* (New York: Harper & Row, 1957).

ment. In turn, neurotic behavior in organizations unquestionably gives rise to more frustration, more failure, more internal conflicts— thus promoting additional neurotic behavior. Nor should this be regarded as something which necessarily interferes with organizational performance. Neurotic drives are often the basis of organizational success. In fact, the large-scale organization often provides the ideal framework within which the neurotic personality—and on rare occasions even the psychotic personality—can attain positions of leadership.

If a serious conflict may exist between the needs of individuals and the demands of organizations, perhaps this conflict extends to the administered society as a whole? Thus Sigmund Freud has suggested that in the modern world culture and civilization may themselves come into conflict with human needs. He thus arrives at the concepts of "social neurosis" and the "pathology of civilized communities."[14]

This theme has been developed further by Fromm, both a follower and a critic of Freud. Fromm [in *The Sane Society*] suggests that in the modern world normalcy itself may be pathological. He holds that the widespread failure to obtain freedom, spontaneity and a genuine expression of self is a "socially patterned defect." He enthusiastically quotes Spinoza's observation that greediness and ambition are forms of departure from sanity. His conclusion is that our over-organized society has become an insane society.

---

[14]Sigmund Freud, *Civilization and Its Discontents* (J. Riviere, tr.; London: Hogarth Press, 1953), pp. 141, 142.

Chapter Four

Reconciling Democracy and Reality

Perhaps you will feel that an alarming picture of American policy-making has been etched in these pages. Surely no American, after years of socialization into democratic ideals, can help but be dismayed at the thought of being "ruled" by elites with interlocking interests and influence. Nor can one be particularly pleased with assuming a coglike function in our bureaucratic society.

Is there a way out? Can we formulate a way to bring the governed, you and me, back into a meaningful dialogue with our governors? Can public policy become more directly responsive to the needs of the citizen, and can the citizen begin to feel the need for more personal involvement in the total policy process?

These are the questions that Richard Goodwin, a former special assistant to Presidents Kennedy and Johnson, formulates and for which he offers several stimulating solutions.

The Shape of American Politics*

Richard N. Goodwin

Over the past several decades much of the world has been experiencing the growing power and dominion of centralized national leadership. The word *nation* itself, having once described a loosely governed confederation of territories or people, now increasingly refers to a fixed geographical area where a central authority assumes mounting responsibility for a range of social and economic activities formerly left to localities, tribal groups, or individuals. Empires have fragmented into nations or, as in Russia and China, old divisions have been obliterated under the imperatives of single rule.

Since this is a modern process, it tends to be most advanced in those countries most firmly committed to industrialization and national power. Africa, on the other hand, still struggles against tribalism, while some Latin American countries battle to assert national authority over historic enclaves of independent power and wealth. It may well appear from a distant point in history that the principal barrier to national progress in our time was simply the lack of a nation. Certainly one reason that many Latin American countries have not developed despite 150 years of independence and a Western heritage is that they have not been countries at all, but collections of independent principalities.

This process of centralization has not been confined by ideology. It has occurred under democracy and dictatorship; it has been guided by capitalism and socialism, communism and fascism. For it is imposed by the fusion of technology with the psychology of power. In making the concentration of power possible and expanding its uses, technology helps to liberate more forceful and sweeping impulses in those individuals who seek authority.

The process is global and differently shaped by the innumerable varieties of culture and circumstance. My discussion, however, will be restricted to the United States. It is what I know, and it best illuminates the most troubling political fact of our age: that the growth in central power has been accompanied by a swift and continual diminution in the significance of the individual citizen, transforming him from a wielder into an object of authority.

Although the problem is larger than politics, I write of it only in that single dimension: one, however, which is steadily more perva-

---

*Reprinted from *Commentary*, by permission; copyright © 1967 by the American Jewish Committee.

sive. Of all human activities, politics—the process of acquiring and using governmental or official power—is among the most responsive to shifting values and situations, always reflecting the dominant and visible themes of the human turbulence which creates it and which it attempts to govern. Hence politics cannot be understood or analyzed apart from the wider society which gives it coloration and direction. An artist may be an age ahead of his time. Even the greatest politician can only be a step or two ahead of his, although important action can spring from his ability to penetrate the obscurity which always enshrouds the real demands of any period. Actions and public words based on a more profound vision than this may suit a prophet, but not a politician. His material is the desires and attitudes of living people, and even the most violent revolutionary cannot escape that constraint, as Lenin knew and Alexander learned.

The growth of central, or federal, power in America during the past few decades has been phenomenal. Only thirty-five years ago, Mencken could write: "The rewards of the presidency are mostly trashy.... The president continues, of course, to be an eminent man, but only in the sense that Jack Dempsey, Babe Ruth, and Henry Ford have been eminent men." He describes a typical presidential day:

> All day long the right hon. lord of us all sits listening to bores and quacks. Anon a secretary rushes in with the news that some eminent movie actor ... has died, and the president must seize a pen and write a telegram of condolence to the widow. Once a year he is repaid by receiving a telegram on his birthday from King George.... It takes four days hard work to concoct a speech without a sensible word in it. Next day a dam must be opened somewhere. Four senators get drunk and try to neck a lady politician. ... The presidential automobile runs over a dog. It rains.

We still mock our presidents, sometimes brutally, but not because they are futile, comic, or unimportant. The springs of today's satire are fear and rage rather than condescension. For the target is immense.

The federal government spends about one-seventh of our national wealth and creates more of it. Between 1950 and 1960, nine out of ten new jobs were created by the public and the private not-for-profit sectors, and only one out of ten by private enterprise. Today, one-third of the entire labor force works for someone other than a profit-making institution. The towering apparatus of scientific and technological research which is remaking our society, and causing apprehension in Europe, is increasingly fueled by federal funds. It is the government, not private business, that is held responsible for the condition of the

economy: credited with prosperity; blamed for recession and infla-
tion; expected simultaneously to make the country prosper, end unemployment, and keep prices down. Of course Washington's power
and skill are not equal to such expectations, but it is inconceivable
that any president today would greet economic dissatisfaction by
pleading, "There is nothing I can do," or even worse, "It is none of my
business." The first to assault any such forfeiture would be the conservative members of the business establishment, rapidly joined in
an improbable chorus by liberal Democrats, the New Left, and the
editors of the *New York Review of Books*.

But today's government is not only expected to maintain prosperity; it is also expected to ensure justice. Those who are denied
their fair demands by our society look to Washington for help in
righting felt wrongs, or scorn it for inaction. The hopeful and contemptuous alike have little doubt where the main responsibility lies.
Social ills, from benighted cities to polluted air, are regarded as the
charge of government; and Washington is also expected to lead the
way out of the automobile-choked tunnels in which we are incarcerat-
ing ourselves.

The 1966 elections dramatized yet another important responsibility now assigned to government: keeper of the status quo. It is
expected to be the protector of all those who are both delighted and
unsure about their new affluence—the suburban houses, new cars, and
television sets. They command the government to restrain any social
turbulence which seems to threaten their personal position. This demand, which might be called Reaganism, finds its most violent expression when it combines with racial fears and bigotry into the "white
backlash." Increasingly, the obligation it imposes conflicts with the
aims of justice and with the more embracing effort to modify society
in the direction of an enlarged individual existence for all.

We have, for the most part, tried to extricate ourselves from this
clash of aims by a kind of tokenism: pretending to make war on poverty or to enforce civil rights while confining resources and power to
a dismally inadequate level, thus easing conscience and subduing
fears while making real sacrifice unnecessary—all often accompanied
by a spurious rhetorical evenhandedness which equates the violence
of a few frustrated Negroes with the huge oppression of millions.
Fortunately the tokenism extends to both sides of the social clash, as
we substitute "wars on crime" or exhortations against "violence" for
more vigorous repression. However, in a relatively nonviolent coun-

try, where the most urgent interests are those of a minority, tokenism is not neutral. It is a powerful ally of existing inequalities.

Augmenting the swelling domestic authority of government, there is the conduct of foreign policy, which gives to a few men, often acting in partial secrecy, the power to commit our country to action in all parts of the world, send hundreds of thousands to fight in distant lands, and entangle the resources and honor of the nation in adventures, promises, programs, and acts in every continent. This control culminates in the numbly familiar power to decree our destruction—a power less real because it is beyond the grasp of consciousness, but present and infusing all the other acts of government with majesty and terror.

We usually associate all this centralization with the presidency, both because the power of that office has increased disproportionately and because the president is most visible to our expectations and our rage: we find a personal target more congenial than an institutional one. Most of our discontents are therefore directed at an individual's defects of character, temperament, or intelligence, rather than at the structure which permits such qualities to rule or, at least, leaves a great deal of our welfare in the hands of chance. The more that power is concentrated, the greater the stakes on the always obscure gamble of selection.

Yet the presidency is not the only part of our government whose power has grown. The Supreme Court helped lead the social revolution of the Negro: an astounding role for an institution whose previous incursions into the political process had nearly always been to check the affirmative action of government (e.g., the New Deal Court, the Income Tax cases, and, more ambiguously, the Dred Scott decision). Sharing in the general euphoria of power, the nine justices of the Supreme Court make major political decisions, unresponsive to the democratic process, in secret meetings on Friday afternoons. Both the number and the scope of such decisions steadily mount. Liberal critics have generally approved this development because they approve the content of the decisions, while the fundamental reshaping of an important institution seems not to trouble them. But it is a transformation which almost certainly will come back to plague us as judicial personnel and social attitudes change, and as an institution which has become more and more political develops an even greater sensitivity to transitory shifts in the political temper.

Congress, too, shares in the mounting power of the federal government, exercising its authority to frustrate the will of the president, or to collaborate with him in denying redress. Congressional action is often spoken of as negative power, a sort of reverse veto. But that is because we are trapped in the liberal rhetoric which defines positive action as increased spending, greater regulation, or new programs. Freed of that semantic trap, we see that the judgments of Congress are extraordinarily powerful affirmative ones: to direct more of our resources toward private consumption than public needs, to cut taxes rather than increase spending, to calm the fears of the homeowner against black invasion, to deny assistance to developing countries, or to support isolationism and chauvinism. At times its judgments are—from a liberal standpoint—more benign, although this is often not perceived, since it tends to take the form of support for the administration. (On the other hand, congressional leaders helped decide that we should stay out of Indochina in 1954, and that the right to some privacy overrode the need to wiretap.) More important than its specific actions is the fact that Congress sets the limits and framework for presidential action. Perhaps the most effective restraint on social legislation, increased spending, and other liberal measures is not any sense of popular opposition, but the foreknowledge that Congress will reject such proposals or that the effort to pass them will eat up so much political capital as to endanger measures thought more essential, or even erode the zealously guarded prestige and power of the president (as in the case of Harry Truman and "socialized" medicine). Presidents would often be far more radical if they thought Congress would let them get away with it. Nor are such assumptions about the limits of congressional tolerance usually made explicit in discussions between congressional leaders and the administration. They are so much a part of the political atmosphere that they dominate and restrict discussion at even the most private meetings. It is not that proposals are rejected. They are not even put forth for analysis or debate; and the process of innovation is one of constantly and cautiously probing these invisible boundaries. Of course, Congress has not shared to any comparable extent in the conduct of foreign affairs. However, the president's concern with foreign matters has probably increased congressional importance in the domestic field since, especially in times of crisis, he must often seek support by moderating his domestic demands, in a sense "buying" allegiance. As most congressmen are far more interested in these issues, they find the division satisfactory.

The reality of increased federal power is undeniable. The events and circumstances which have created it are more tangled and ambiguous. Most obvious is the necessity for federal leadership in the conduct of foreign affairs, accepted by even the most conservative. Thus, as America became a global power with swiftly spreading burdens and ambitions, government waxed. Our relations with other countries, deeply and even mortally consequential in themselves, inevitably seep into a hundred areas of national life, shaping the structure of our industrial system, setting priorities for education and scholarship, pushing us toward technology and away from other pursuits.

Through this indirect effect on other institutions, and through the immediate impact of particular decisions and acts, the conduct of foreign affairs pervades the attitudes of the nation, contributing to a national mood of enthusiasm or resignation, anger or despair, which unavoidably carries over into a wide range of unrelated public problems and private sensibilities. The war in Vietnam has crippled and drained the drive behind civil rights. The presence and potential of nuclear power has entered into our art, and probably into the psychological structure of every citizen. Yet this towering power is for the most part in the hands of a single man and his employees. Even the normal checks on public dissent are partially sterilized by ignorance, central control over information, and the fact that immediate self-interest is usually not involved, thus depriving protest of the passion which comes from simple personal engagement. It is part of the naivete of the conservative position to believe that foreign affairs can be compartmentalized—that enormous power can be granted in the world arena while being withdrawn from domestic affairs. The truth is that authority over foreign affairs carries with it a new, wholly modern, ability to alter the nature and direction of our society.

In some measure the increase in central power is attributable to the converging flow of historical and psychological factors. The New Deal, out of necessity, created large new authority for government. More importantly, it led citizens to expect a great deal more than they previously had from Washington. Once this process had begun, it could not easily be arrested. For the natural inertia of the American system resists all but the most critical and revolutionary conditions, such as the Depression itself. The single conservative administration since Roosevelt could only consolidate, and not reverse, the flow. In our nation popular expectations and political power ride side by side. As demands increased, the central government was compelled to seek fresh authority. Those who chose conservative principle over political response met the fate of Taft and Goldwater.

Strengthening this domestic "revolution of rising expectations" is the natural tendency of political leaders to add to their power, to relish the "anguish" of decision, and to resent any effort to oppose their will. I do not mean this as criticism. It is a psychological condition of great leadership to want power and receive satisfaction from its exercise, just as a great artist must desire command over his materials. (Justice [Felix] Frankfurter once told me no one could be a great president who didn't enjoy the job—even if he was occasionally tormented by its burdens. Of course, the fact that a man enjoys power does not in itself make him great.) It is natural for a leader, once in possession of power, to resist frustration. Our system is deliberately and instinctively designed to restrain this ominous psychological inclination. The great number of institutional "checks and balances" are combined with less formal limitations grounded in national traditions and values, political realities, popular sentiment, and the power of the press to criticize and expose. These are often the most potent restraints, not only limiting what a leader can do, but what he would think of doing. They are accepted and even cherished by men whose indoctrination in the American system is stronger than inner drives to power. Like most important political guides, they are rarely articulated, having been absorbed into character and personality. (For example, no one doubted that President Truman would relinquish the steel industry when the Supreme Court ordered him to do so. Yet it is hard to think of another country where a president would yield to a judicial body on a matter of such magnitude. Nor could the Court have made him act if he refused to. It was simply "unthinkable" that he should refuse.)

The price of this system is often inaction, or very slow progress. For radical and swift changes require great and concentrated authority, which, in turn, is extraordinarily dangerous in the wrong hands. We can see today how the concentration of power over foreign affairs in a single man—long a goal of that liberal thought which was contemptuous of congressional conservatism—has dissolved the normal checks of our institutional structure. And these restraints have been neutralized precisely in the area where political checks—public opinion and the press—are weakest, poorly informed, most prone to emotional reaction (especially since personal economic interests are rarely affected in any obvious way), and most willing, in resigned bafflement at complexities, to accept presidential direction on faith. It is possible that conservatives have something to teach about the value of institutional arrangements, and the unwisdom of sacrificing them to immediate desires. At least we should understand that the hope for pure self-restraint in the use of power can be a very feeble guarantee, and often weakest in the temperament which wishes to accomplish the most for the country.

This interlocking psychological and historical process has been given a greater momentum by our increasing ability to shape events from the center. Economics and, to a far lesser extent, other social sciences have enabled us to achieve an improved mastery over the operations of society. We now try to control economic conditions in every section of the country, using newly refined tools of fiscal and monetary policy—raising and lowering taxes and interest rates in response to computerized projection and the counsel of experts and businessmen. (These tools are more doubtful than a few recent successes have led us to believe, and as presently used they have serious social costs, depriving the government of revenue to support needed social programs and generally aggravating maldistribution of income.) Mass communications and swift transportation have enabled government to bring its authority and assistance to bear in a detailed and specific manner, allowing it to construct the rapidly responsive bureaucracy hitherto thought impossible in a nation of continental dimensions, and encouraging the natural tendency of local officials to turn to the federal government. Hardly a day passes without a phone call from a mayor asking for concrete advice or help. Task forces and experts are constantly dispatched to states and towns, not only in flood or famine, but to examine housing programs, evaluate complaints about pollution control, and to decide whether new power lines are going to blight a suburban area. Computerization of government, the next stage, will increase the possibilities of central control and influence and, unless we make some fairly radical structural changes, will in fact bring about such an increase.

Many of these new mechanisms and techniques are more efficient and result in greater justice—at least in the abstract sense of that term. It is hard to argue that we should not make sure everyone pays his taxes. Yet the knowledge that a giant computer in West Virginia is making a detailed analysis of the economic status of every American will add an inevitable, subtle, and pervasive tension to the financial transactions of each citizen—just as the sight of a police car in the rear-view mirror makes even the law-abiding motorist wary and self-conscious. That is a rather high price to pay to catch a few cheaters, especially when our tax laws give advantages to the privileged which no system of automation can remedy.

Access and communication, however, also work in reverse, occasionally yielding a political influence to disadvantaged groups greater than their economic and social power. We are past the time of the 1920's when millions of farmers could languish in desperation and cause scarcely a ripple in Washington. For example, the civil rights movement owes much of its impact to the television cameras which displayed the cruelties of Bull Connor and the violence of Selma to an audience for whom racial injustice in the South had seemed as remote as apartheid in South Africa. Through modern communication, Negro leaders have become national celebrities, enhancing the power and possibilities of leadership. Similarly, the poverty program owes a great deal to books and articles: a series in the *New York Times* on Kentucky, Michael Harrington's book, and a piece by Dwight Macdonald in the *New Yorker*—all of which helped to stimulate conscience and political action by introducing thoughtful citizens and national leaders to the agonies of the previously unnoticed millions trapped beneath the surface of affluence.

These varied forces contributing to central power have a unifying theme: the mutually reinforcing concurrence of national demand and expectation with the assertion of power and the capacity to exercise it. There is, however, a more subtle, pervasive, and probably more significant factor. It is the gradual dissolution of alternative outlets for grievances, demands, ambitions, and inner needs. It is as if many small magnets and a single large one were scattered on a floor. If the smaller magnets steadily lose their force, particles would break away and take their place in the stronger field of force. Something like that has happened to American political life.

There are, after all, many ways for a man to change the conditions of his life or modify his environment. He can act through local government, social institutions, and private organizations. Or he can gain access to opportunities which do not rest on official action—by, for example, "going West" to an unsettled frontier.

All these possibilities have been dissolving. Large-scale opportunity outside settled institutions began to disappear when the West was closed. After that, migrants and minorities sought a path into society through unskilled labor. Its virtual elimination in modern times may prove as momentous an event as the end of the frontier. Certainly the distress of northern Negroes, and their struggle, would have taken a different shape if this same opportunity had been open to them. Today it is no longer possible to avoid conflict with society while gathering strength to force an entrance. The confrontation must be direct and immediate, and the unequal odds in such a clash require the intervention of the federal government, now the necessary agent of social change—and thus more powerful still.

More important to the growth of central power than the destruction of frontiers is the dwindling influence of local government and private associations. This erosion has been produced by two major social changes. The first, and most obvious, is the enormous resistance and complexity of many modern problems, requiring an antagonist of great force and resources. The second is a loss of connection: the fraying of human, civic, and territorial bonds between the individual and the disembodied structures which surround him. In consequence, the individual loses confidence in the capacity of local structures to modify the political conditions of existence, a self-fulfilling distrust which accelerates the weakening process. Diminishing faith turns people, not away from authority, but toward a more powerful center. This is certainly one of the reasons that totalitarianism finds its moment of opportunity at times of relative chaos.

Added to the many social and psychological conditions which have assaulted these historic structures are the growth in population (diluting participation in local government) and our fantastic mobility (making it hard to retrain local allegiances). Therefore, individuals again turn toward the central government where, it seems, grievances and hopes can be effectively aired, and to which citizens in all parts of the country, even the rootless and displaced, feel some connection.

These weakened structures confront a social order whose growing rigidity closes off many traditional non-governmental outlets for change and for those personal ambitions which depend on social justice. The power of large corporations, the sanctity of the search for profits, the desirability of swift economic growth (we measure our success by our Gross National Product), and the exaltation of technology, are all virtually beyond serious challenge. Private citizens, communities, and even states feel helpless to deal with abuses resulting from an unchallengeable ideology and, being small, they are most vulnerable to the interests which benefit from this ideology. Thus our suburbs become horrors of ugliness, discomfort, and spiritual devastation because the right to buy land and build on it is sacred. The blurred advance of technology makes it impossible for any but the most sophisticated and endowed to weigh the advantage of change against the social ills it may bring. Since so much of our system is fixed, it is necessary to turn to the one authority still capable of channeling our institutions, through coercion or guidance, toward desired change: the central government.

Rising wealth also adds to central power. Although new affluence encourages conservatism, the "new conservatives" are usually far more concerned with the content of authority than the fact of its exercise. They find it possible to oppose welfare programs on the ground that they are against big government while supporting larger police powers and a range of new coercive authority for the state. In addition, many modern conservatives favor an interventionist and aggressive foreign policy which would inevitably lead to more formidable and sweeping powers for the federal government. This is far less principled than the conservatism of Jefferson or even Taft. It is rooted in economic self-interest, but whereas the dominant emotion of classical New England conservatives was confidence in themselves and in local institutions coupled with resentment at intrusion, the dominant feeling behind much of the new conservatism is fear (reinforced by a temperamental preference for abstraction over compassion). Behind the paradoxical conservative contribution to growing central power is the desire for protection of the newly affluent against unpleasant, troubling, and threatening social forces. Much of the root of today's liberal–conservative tension is the clash between fear and confidence, which is why conservatism tends to rise in times of felt danger and crisis. Certainly some of the most successful reactionary and conservative movements have rested on uncertainty and apprehension, while liberalism has generally tried to fuse popular desires with elitist confidence. (This gives us some hope that the second and later generations of the newly affluent—even in California—will be less conservative.)

Central power is not in itself contemptible or hazardous, but must be judged by the extent to which it enlarges or constricts the possibilities of individual existence. Difficult as it is to untangle relationships and sources, we can be certain that rising central power has been accompanied by the diminishing significance of political man. In part this human lessening flows from the increase in central power itself; in part from the changes contributing to that increase; and, in incalculable part, from the general nature of the modern world.

The individual's confidence in his own significance rests on the share of mastery he possesses over his life and environment. An internal ability to come to terms with the world, to seek a place in the drama, is imperative. Still, even the most intense and controlled awareness of self will not suffice for the person who is constantly denied, rejected, and ignored by his world, unless he possesses those rare inner resources which allow him to create his own. But that is not politics. As political affairs become more centralized and as personal, group, and local responsibilities are absorbed, this vital sense of mastery is eroded. For, in fact, the individual's ability to control circumstances is diminished.

This is not simply a political phenomenon. It saturates our philosophical, technological, and social environment; and even as politics, it cannot be discussed apart from the commanding values of the time. These values differ radically from those which in one form or another have been dominant since the Renaissance—a historical moment, Michelet explained, that was characterized by "man's discovering of the world and of man." Before this, Burckhardt says, man had seen himself as a part of a series of categories —a member of his people, party, or family. Now "man became a spiritual individual." As this focus shifted, there was an effort to comprehend the essence of man, along with a search for a fresh synthesis of the new "spiritual individual" with the world around him. There was a growing faith that incomplete human understanding resulted from an imperfect knowledge we could labor to complete.

One of the last glories of the Renaissance, and one of its destroyers, Albert Einstein, when faced with theories that assumed the essential role of chance in describing the existence of basic units of the material world, asked: "Do you really believe God resorts to dice playing?" He spoke in the tradition which encouraged the conviction that the free play of the inquiring mind would lead to a complete and harmonious account of reality. In that tradition philosophers and artists alike had struggled to grasp man's nature as incorporated into systematic statements of faith and organic representations of reality. Now the belief in the possibility of such unity and wholeness is fading. We live, instead, at a time of fragmentation and dissection, in search of the components of our sensible world. The concept of God as a source of moral authority dissolves into mystical generalizations or disappears. Efforts at systematic philosophy are scorned, ignored, or become the province of esoteric technicians. Saint Augustine and Spinoza become Norman O. Brown and Marshall McLuhan.

Art continues and reflects the process of fragmentation, reducing objects to light and form and regarding constituent elements as ultimate realities rather than as parts of a large reconstruction. In literature and films we dissect emotions and actions alike, casting them as isolated fragments in order to evoke confused sadness at absurdity. Our hunger is more for experience than for meaning, for expanded sensation rather than coherent understanding. Even the insistent quest for the nature and meaning of man begins to yield, as psychology and biochemistry break us up into instincts, drives, creations of other beings, molecules, chemical codes, and electrical patterns, until the question, *What is man?*, begins to lose meaning in its historic sense. Man becomes a physical phenomenon, different from other forms of life only in degree and power, all his complexities ultimately describable and predictable. We look for the truth in the pieces of the puzzle and not in the picture they make. For that picture is largely the random, purposeless assembly of myriad components in a single unit of living flesh.

This drive away from system and toward fragmentation has the force of a primitive religion. No one denies that it must go on, or that science and technology are to be pursued regardless of the values they imperil. *They* are the values. At one time it was possible to ask whether the fact that the earth revolved around the sun was worth knowing, if knowing it might deprive us of God. But it is Galileo who is our hero, not his foes.

Our American culture, more intensely than any other, reflects the process of fragmentation. A man as perceptive as André Malraux can claim that the United States lacks a national culture, since he looks for that culture in its classical sense—a structure of values and meaning embodying itself in certain forms. Our culture is of a different kind, rooted in our history as a nation. It is a culture of restlessness. Its principal values are change and movement, all continuously feeding the hunger for experience. This culture is sweeping the world, in painting, in theater, in the changing beat of music, in the adoration of technology. It is the culture of an age of fragmentation, at once reflecting and feeding that process. For it does not demand or provide the resting-place that unity and wholeness require. It transforms values into psychology, drives, hungers, and actions; it replaces belief with "authenticity."

Whatever this process of fragmentation may yield us in scientific knowledge or artistic accomplishment, it is charged with danger for political and social man. In these arenas of human activity there is no possible unit smaller than the individual. And the most vital and passionate need of the individual is for mastery: both over himself, and through some shaping share in the world around him. It becomes enormously difficult to achieve such mastery in the midst of dissolution and constant movement. Yet those who are deprived of mastery for themselves are often driven to cede it to others, perhaps ultimately forfeiting their freedom.

Whether or not the foregoing description has psychological and philosophical validity, it provides an analytic lens through which we can view our political and social institutions. More conservative than science or thought, they still reflect—as already suggested in the above account of the forces behind rising central power—the more profound contemporary currents of fragmentation and dissolution. Family ties stretch and break as the gap between the experience of the generations widens, and as more spacious possibilities of geographical and occupational mobility remove the pressure to reconcile natural hostilities and make it easier to indulge them. The community disappears, as the comprehensible unit of living blends into the huge, accidental monstrosities our cities have become. Science describes our world in terms beyond all but the most specialized understanding, dissolving control in mystery. Most of us know little more about the working of our world than did the ancients who ascribed natural phenomena to spirits. They, however, had the advantage of believing in their explanation, while we are only aware of our ignorance. Cities and technology, production and population, grow and change, powered by forces which seem beyond the control, and even the desire, of the individual person. A handful of men in remote capitals hold our existence hostage to their wisdom or impulse or sanity. The small groups where we could once achieve a sense of belonging and of being needed, because we could encompass them with our knowledge and presence, are disappearing, while the activities they once guided—the life of a town and of its citizens —now seem hopelessly beyond their competence.

As these myriad enemies assault the private stronghold of influence and importance, alienation, rage, desperation, and a growing sense of futility increasingly scar our political life. Two principal forms of reaction emerge. Violent protests and extreme convictions reflect the frustration of many at their inability to assert their significance and to share in the enterprise of society. Men of vitality and passion matched against indifference and encumbered by futility have virtually no recourse but rage. The history of the civil rights movement reveals how helplessness can drive the pursuit of unexceptionable goals toward violent rhetoric. *Black power* is more a cry of despair and a plea for attention than a signal for battle. Among larger numbers, less endowed with vitality and conviction, there is a rising determination to protect and conserve. They seek security for their present position in the face of receding confidence in their own ability to shape the future.

We see these basic impulses in manifold, sometimes terrifying, forms: more reasonably in the New Right and the New Left, irrationally violent among Minutemen and John Birchers, Black Muslims and southern secessionists. They are reflected in the compulsive search for a hero or an enemy, and in a deepening disgust with political life itself. (Nothing more ironically illuminates this point than the contrasting attitudes toward power in *MacBird* and in the Shakespearean plays of which it is a pastiche.) All these conflicting movements help serve the single purpose of giving the individuals who belong to them the inner sense of significance that comes from being a part of some larger purpose. They reveal how a feeling of impotence is charged with danger, polarizing groups and individuals and creating a nation of strangers, until even those with whom we sympathize glare at us across an impassable barrier of hostility. The gradual decline of the Vietnam debate into competing slogans and invective is our most recent example of this process in action. The result is not merely extremism, but resignation and lassitude embodied in an unwillingness to face problems, make personal commitments, or to act until difficulties have all but overwhelmed us.

Thus, whatever our particular political positions, the one overriding goal of political life must be to help restore and strengthen that faith of the individual in himself which is the source of national direction and generosity of deed.

This may be an illusory goal. Perhaps the machine is already out of control, hurling us toward a future where we will all blend into some grotesque organism, our sensations absorbed by discordant sound and flashing light—where life itself is an endless "trip." Yet no one who pursues the profession of politics can permit himself to regard the goal as illusory, any more than a novelist can permit himself to believe that the form in which he works is obsolete. Politics alone cannot remedy a condition whose causes are so manifold. But it is at least partly a political task.

II

There are two mingled aspects of public policy: content and technique, and though they are ultimately inseparable, each has effects of its own. The United States, Russia, and China, for example, have all worked to increase agricultural production, but their differing techniques have shaped the life of the individual farmer in drastically different ways. Thus political methods and structures can in certain cases do more to affect the individual than the substance of policy itself. But before proposing some structural changes in a form concrete and specific enough for immediate political action, I would like to touch briefly on the matter of substance.

The content of public policy in any society is dictated by ideology; there is no such thing as a non-ideological society. All nations, including our own, are governed on the basis of ideas and values, passionately shared and defended, which are not derived either from the necessities of nature or the command of God. If a man snatches his hand from a hot stove, that is not ideological. If he then decrees there shall be no more hot stoves in order to prevent burning, he has imposed an ideology (and one wholly alien to our own). Public affairs cannot be conducted outside an ideological system. *Pragmatism*, as we tend to use that word, may be adequate for a man stranded on a desert island—at least once he has decided to live and seek rescue. Our own world is too complex for that. We cannot hope to grasp all the variables of our life and deal with them anew each time we struggle for decision. We need, and we have, a mixed array of beliefs, values, and ideas to serve as reference points, so that pragmatic action moves carefully within a tightly confined ideological space.

Ours is one of the most ideological nations of all. The very absence of serious and widespread public debate proves how successfully ideas have been woven into our national life. They almost seem part of the nature of things rather than what they are: human choices among a great variety of possibilities. There are many ways to resolve difficulties, but only ideology can reveal what a difficulty is. The elements of our ideology, not the illusory question of its existence, require careful exploration by those who seek change and reform. I make no such ambitious effort here. Yet some of these elements are obvious: nationalism and the democratic process, concepts of individual liberty and obedience to law, the faith in technology and the pursuit of invention, the virtue of rising national wealth, the willingness to reward production more than teaching, or acting more than contemplation, and even the conviction that problems can be solved.

Anyone in government who has had the experience of proposing measures which even cautiously probe the boundaries of our system of belief can testify to the rooted passion which defends it. Often changes that are self-evidently beneficial prove surprisingly hard to bring about even when opposing interests are pitifully weak. When we find that a series of such obstructed reforms has a single theme, we have touched an ideological nerve. Therefore the search for policies which might enhance the individual's sense of mastery must, in the first instance, be ideological. The only realistic political approach is to build on major elements of existing belief rather than to erase and begin again.

In our domestic affairs, two ideas above all need to be modified and strengthened. One is our idea of justice. The other is the concept of public responsibility for the quality of individual life.

Justice, as equal treatment, or in the more abstract sense of the fulfillment of fair expectations, is a historic goal of the American system. It has generally been enforced by the elimination of formal barriers—property restrictions on voting, racial and religious discrimination—on the assumption that in the absence of such barriers, disadvantaged individuals and groups would be free to fight and work their way into the society according to their individual merits. This idea is no longer adequate; indeed, it has itself become a principal obstacle to justice. For many of the weapons of earlier battles have been seriously blunted.

The classic pathway of unskilled labor is now closed to the excluded. Their potential political strength has been mortally diluted by the rise of metropolitan populations (making their numbers less important), and by the shift in power toward a central government which must weigh their needs against the demands of a huge majority—something mayors of Boston never had to do. The complexities of modern existence are an ever returning maze through which the underprivileged must wander in mounting frustration: bad education breeds unemployment, unemployment brings poverty, poverty dulls capacity and desire, which in turn insures poor education. The spread of affluence requires minorities to battle, not against a small entrenched aristocracy, but a huge and ever more fearful majority. The essence of social struggle has always been *Which side are you on?* and the sides are becoming steadily more disproportionate. The Negro in particular must also face the darkly resistant racial feelings which are more intense than the hostility ever directed against other American minorities. All this commands government to go beyond the responsibility for an often illusory equality of "opportunity," and to get itself the job of equipping underprivileged individuals to meet the demands of society while at the same time compelling their admittance. Justice is not merely liberation, but assistance and compulsion. This does not entail a change in expressed American objectives but a shift in the ideas essential to those objectives.

Clashing even more dramatically with the old ideologies is the necessity for government to concern itself with the quality of individual life. In a few carefully confined areas we have made this our concern. The Bill of Rights was not adopted for its economic efficiency, and the conservation struggle is a half-century old. Still, the major goal of our modern domestic policy has been rising national wealth and its wider distribution, with special provision for those kept from competition by unavoidable circumstance—the old, unemployed, and afflicted. These are benign objectives, but they are dismally insufficient. The assumption that private affluence would enable individual citizens to create a descent and liberating environment has collapsed. That failure can be seen in the chaos and degradation of our cities, the pollution of our air and water, the ruthless destructiveness of our highways, and the desolation of our countryside. The same qualitative failure pursues us into every corner of our national life, whether we are hypnotized by the destructive sterility of our government-supported (but not controlled) television networks, or send our children to schools which crush imagination and the desire to learn. Even the sustaining values of community have, in incalculable measure, been destroyed, not by changing values, but by a physical environment designed to obstruct continuing human contact.

The important thing about these afflictions is that virtually no one can escape them. Certainly so many problems with a common theme must have an ideological base—a suspicion strengthened by the knowledge that effort directed at such social ills would rapidly return to enrich the nation, not only spiritually, but in dollars and cents. We would create jobs and useful work and investment, finding it possible to have both private affluence and public improvement. The strength of the obstructing ideology here can be gauged by the fact that, until recently, we not only failed to attack these problems, but rarely thought of doing so. Made invisible by ideological preconceptions, the entire issue hardly reached the level of public debate (though, of course, some social critics saw the problem).

This ideology sets the boundary line between those matters which are the proper concern of government and those which rest with individuals. The barrier is rooted in a passion which transcends immediate self-interest—and we can all think of activities unrelated to economic interests which we wish kept free of government. In this case ideology dictated that commercial enterprise had a right to expand and change. Of course abuses should be restrained. But they were abuses of economic power directed against consumers and citizens—monopolies and price-fixing, child labor and resistance to unions. Abuse was a category which did not encompass the non-economic, social consequences of economic expansion. These were in effect forbidden ground. Once personal liberty was ensured, the proper concern of government was economic expansion, protection against commercial exploitation, and justice as narrowly defined. As if this concept were not confining enough, there were also the inherent limitations of a political system designed to respond to crisis. We could act only when a problem became urgent or an abuse widespread, provoking intense public concern. We had neither the mechanisms nor the habits of thought for any other approach; and except for some rudimentary and permissive economic planning (which fits the ideology), the deficiency remains. Unfortunately, when many of today's social problems reach the crisis stage they are already almost beyond redemption: New York City.

It is now essential to accept the reality that the public conditions of private life are a matter of public concern, that dealing with them is beyond the capacities of individual citizens, and that they require a major redirection of our energies and resources. The choice between lower taxes and a vast program for the cities is ordinarily posed in terms of the vague and ideologically potent stereotypes of government spending and bureaucracy as against private consumption and initiative. It is natural for citizens, confronted by such a choice, to prefer immediate tangible reward to remote and largely abstract benefit. In truth, it is all private consumption: the choice is between a second car and clean air, between a new television set and a park for one's children. When we spend billions for space while slums go unattended, and when we lavish attention on computer systems to guide aircraft while breathing poisoned air, we are not simply being wasteful or irrational; we are acting out of a structure of ideas whose modification requires national leadership and education. The time is propitious for such a change, precisely because the affluence which has been created by our old policies allows people to divert themselves from the economic struggle long enough to feel dismay at the world we have been building.

There are already some signs of a shift in belief. We have new demonstration programs for our cities and even a Council on the Arts. Just as this movement began to pick up momentum, it was paralyzed by the Vietnamese war. If times improve, we can hope for an ideological change bringing the demand for public action against those social ills which cripple the quality of individual life. We may eventually view the refusal of a builder to provide parks and trees with the same incredulity with which we would now greet a denial by General Motors of Walter Reuther's right to bargain for higher wages—an idea easily accepted not too long ago.

Utopian as much of this may sound, it is less far-reaching than the changes required in our policies toward the rest of the world. However, in foreign policy the possibility of radical changes in ideology—and consequently in action—is far greater. Our domestic policies are sustained by a network of resistant structures and institutions, closely identified with the personal self-interest of large and powerful numbers. Foreign policy, on the other hand, is much less firmly tied to group interests or to institutional structures. That is why it can change so rapidly, and why the president has such great power in this area. We have moved from isolation to war, from a relapsing withdrawal to the Marshall Plan, from Kennedy detente to Johnson interventionism, with each shift eventually winning much establishment and popular assent.

Another reason for directing major concentration to foreign affairs is their importance. Our great problems increasingly derive from world conditions. It is on the world stage that America has its opportunity to act a great role in human history—an enterprise to alter the human condition and the relationship among the peoples of the earth.

Such an enterprise is essential to the goal of an enlarged individual existence, and thus to our national health and sanity. Personal fulfillment flows from the opportunity to share in a great adventure, whose aim and conduct can be a source of idealistic pride. A gifted and lucky few find this in their own work and talents. For most of us, nothing is more oppressive than to be a member of a society whose operations we view as menial, self-regarding, cruel, or aimless. Today, especially among the young, the inspiring sense Americans have had of helping to unfold a noble destiny is fading. Still, even in the harshest criticism there is an undertone of hope which would be impossible in many other more cynical and less powerful countries (their impotence is real). Behind the most passionate contemporary assaults against modern America, we can glimpse the unarticulated belief that with other leaders or with a different system, this country—its people—is still capable of constructive and idealistic action. I share this optimism.

Clearly such a shift in foreign policy cannot be brought about solely by the desire of a rich and powerful country to protect itself from global turbulence—the foreign counterpart of the new conservatism. There is no glory, and little future, in being the guardian of the international status quo. But neither is it necessary to be self-damaging. For we are in the almost unique position where a policy of revolutionary idealism is consistent with our own immediate self-interest as it is most deeply understood.

Before exploring this point, let us clear away some underbrush. People and nations can, and often do, act with irrational lust and violence. Our society and its values have been threatened by military aggression in the past, and may well be again. There are those who would joyfully overrun us tomorrow if they could. Sometimes it may be necessary to resist by force, and it is certainly necessary to be prepared for such resistance. Until there are important changes in the human condition, fear, not love or even reason, will be a principal keeper of the peace. (I am not talking here of our disastrous policy in Vietnam.) It is also true that particular problems require concrete or *pragmatic* responses. However, cult words like *realism* or *pragmatism* should not be allowed to cloud the real problems of foreign policy. They are not wrong, but they are virtually useless. All they mean is that any objective should be pursued rationally and with the widest possible knowledge of the circumstances. They tell us nothing about the objectives which should be pursued.

Self-interest is another word used to confuse and often destroy debate. The physical protection of our population and its material well-being are clearly in our self-interest. Beyond that are multitudinous complications of values and judgment. As between tranquility or ferment, indulgence or sacrifice, the comfort of undisturbed and mounting wealth or the joy of living by ideals, it is far from self-evident which we ought to choose, and our choice will rest on the spiritual circumstances of the country. However, there is a second and more corrupting sense in which the term "self-interest" is used—to label particular actions and policies. This usage is almost always invoked to end debate entirely, serving as it does to imply that an adversary is hopelessly abstract, romantic, or confused. Thus we are told that it is in our self-interest to destroy the Vietcong, or to support the military in certain South American countries, or to be gentle with South Africa. (Conservatives seem to have a genius for winning the all-important semantic battles. Anti-union laws become "right to work"; national health insurance becomes "socialized medicine"; a proposal to eliminate the concentration of the draft on the poor and disadvantaged becomes a "lottery.") Those who oppose such policies are often cast by this brilliant rhetorical device as betrayers of the national interest.

Yet those policies are not expressions of self-interest at all, but only measures which someone thinks will contribute to it. Moreover, the self-interest they presume to advance is often narrow and short-sighted. To take a simple and obvious example: there are those who wish us to support, or at least readily accept, authoritarian military governments in South America because they contribute to economic and political stability. I believe we should support liberal, progressive forces in South America, even if they are revolutionary in character (I do not becloud the issue by introducing the subject of communism), because in the long run they are the only force which can both win in their own countries and maintain a fruitful association with the United States; because we will be more comfortable and (again in the long run), safer in a hemisphere dominated by these forces; and because our spiritual health as a country will be enhanced by supporting them. Thus I view my position as realistically and pragmatically in our self-interest, and I look upon favoring the military as a form of self-destructive and quixotic remanticism.

Of course, a general policy is not a detailed guide to specific problems. If the military takes over, its rule becomes a fact which must be dealt with, introducing many complicated questions to be weighed on their own. Nevertheless, the general proposition gives a direction to policies and expressions which will be profoundly significant to ultimate results and will often also have a crucial effect on particular decisions. (Thus, we cut off aid to Peru for two years because it had a dispute with a Standard Oil subsidiary over the division of royalties. That action flowed from a distinct ideological position that was violently opposed to our true interests. A different, and more intelligent, understanding of our goals in Peru would have forbidden such a masochistic decision.) In short, the imperative questions of foreign policy are: which goals serve the long-run interest of the American people, and what policies are best calculated to move us in that direction. That discussion leads from the most remote and prophetic considerations to specific policies and acts. For example, we can assert that we wish to help in the development of the Third World. Why? Out of charity or fear? Do we really have an obligation? If so, what is it grounded on? Do we believe that the world can't exist with a poor majority and a rich minority? Why not, when it always has? If we should help, then how much, whom, and under what conditions?

Answers to such questions are implied in the view that a policy of revolutionary idealism is both desirable and practicable for the United States. To begin with, there is the comforting reality that we are almost the first great power whose self-aggrandizement does not depend on dominion over others. Our enormous strength makes us impregnable to any but the largest and most serious threats—for the moment only to a direct attack by the Soviet Union. China may, in some still remote time, be able to transform hostility into danger, but Cuba, Guinea, Albania, etc., unless they should become active and effective agents of a hostile great power, are only an emotional annoyance.

Our economy is also virtually self-sufficient, depending for mounting prosperity neither on control of foreign markets nor on foreign sources of raw materials. So long as conditions permit us to buy and sell in the world market, we need not exercise control or ownership over any other territory. It is true that our gold reserves are in a hazardous position—which, however, could be secured if we were willing to free ourselves from the theology of international finance. In any event that particular danger, real and influential on policy as it now is, does not rest on reality, in the sense that it does not come from any weakness of our economy. It is a creature of habits and conventions which, if changed, would not affect our ability to produce or consume.

The bald statement of these facts does conceal several complexities. For example, the spread of hostile governments to significant areas of the world would have a profound and damaging psychological effect, even if it did not place us in direct physical danger. The facts do, however, make it plain that our foreign policy is potentially freer from the bedrock considerations of national security and economic health than that of any other power in history.

This relative freedom gives us an opportunity to pursue a foreign policy which can engage the pride and idealism of our own people, enhancing their well-being and lifting the quality of our civilization with vastly liberating effects on future generations. The American people are not only willing to support such a policy, but need it. It is no accident that President Kennedy's best remembered line is the famous "Ask not..." or that the Peace Corps received such an overwhelmingly unexpected response. Leadership which appeals to confidence instead of fear will find a great thirst for idealistic mission among the majority. It has been present in times of war, and there is much evidence, especially on college campuses, that it is waiting to be slaked today.

Much of our present foreign-policy debate revolves around clashing espousals of isolationism. They are new types of isolationism, since our strength, our world position, and the decline of other powers make the old style impossible. On one side, to oversimplify, are those who wish our policy to be directed basically at opposition to real or apprehended physical threats. The twin elements of this view are containment and order. Its underlying plea is, "Leave us alone." On the other side are those who believe we have no right to influence other countries or to interfere in their affairs. This view is often accompanied by a disbelief in the reality of irrational passions, hatreds, and desires for conquest (except, perhaps, when it comes to the United States). Its plea is, "Leave *them* alone."

But there is also a non-isolationist strain in American history and culture—a sense of American mission—upon which we can draw. Certainly we cannot presume to dictate how the nations of the world should organize their societies. But we do have something to offer and to teach. We know that it is better for people to eat than to starve and that increasing individual prosperity is better than hopeless misery. We know that human well-being is increased by liberty of expression and belief, and damaged by repression and persecution. Peace is better than war, and the growth of effective international restraints is a necessary condition of peace.

Propositions of this type (and many more are possible) seem self-evident, even banal. So they are—until they are coupled with the assertion that the United States has a responsibility to realize them on a global scale. To the extent that we act on them now, it is in a token and fragmentary way; therefore, for all the rhetoric, they are not an important part of our foreign policy.

A foreign policy grounded on *this* ideology would look far different from much of our present conduct. We would devote large resources to the economic development of the poorer countries. We would alter the patterns of trade to encourage world-wide industrialization. We would direct our support and friendship to those nations trying to create such conditions, regardless of their shifting political attitudes, unless they were to rise to the status of a real and physically menacing enemy. We would take the lead in mobilizing serious international opposition to large-scale persecution and oppression, and not be content to regard an occasional vote for a diluted United Nations resolution against apartheid as a triumph of idealistic liberalism. We would recognize that revolutionary violence may sometimes be necessary to eliminate deeply embedded institutions and values which obstruct both justice and progress.

None of these policies, or the turbulence they might often help create, would—except in very special and unusual circumstances—endanger either our security or our economy. On the contrary, they would contribute to the emergence of a community of shared values and expectations within which we would undoubtedly be safer and more prosperous than ever. It would be our kind of world. The forceful pursuit of such policies would have an impact on the spiritual welfare of American society which would radiate into every aspect of our domestic affairs. We would stand for something, not just rhetorically but in engagement, and that sort of ideology would generate its own consequences in action.

A foreign policy of this kind would represent realism in its clearest and noblest form. To sacrifice basic beliefs and goals to the apparent demands and interests of every passing problem and conflict reflects both timidity and lack of imagination. In the long run such a course can only lead to a world environment in which even our narrowest material and physical interests are unsafe, to say nothing of its inevitably erosive effect on the idea of American civilization itself. We are fond of historical parallels. They should convince us that in the conditions of the modern world a policy founded on generosity and idealism is the only policy that is pragmatic and realistic, conducive to national grandeur and, ultimately, to national survival.

III

As important as the content and direction of public policies are the methods and structures used to carry them out. Initially, the elaborate structure of American federalism mirrored the judgment that a great deal should be left to local authority. For decades we have been moving in the other direction. Not only is this a dangerous and, as I believe, a mistaken course, but it is becoming clearer that certain substantive objectives utterly depend upon fashioning fresh techniques. Modern poverty, for example, cannot be abolished by friendly edicts from remote officials, and even if it could, the result would be sterile, vacuous, and purely material.

The blended goal of structure and policy alike must be to meet specific ills through methods which can in themselves enlarge the sense and reality of individual relevance and participation. The way to accomplish this, at least on the political front, is through decentralization—by assisting and compelling states, communities, and private groups to assume a greater share of responsibility for collective action. In other words, both burden and enterprise must be shifted into units of action small enough to allow for more intimate personal contact and numerous enough to widen the outlets for direct participation and control.

Such a shift, although it faces many problems, is both the most practical and politically realistic of all the ideas discussed here. From the community action program of the war against poverty to the private organizing efforts of Students for a Democratic Society, we are being given tangible proof of the viability of the decentralized approach. If these programs have been inadequate, it is only because they have so far been unable to overcome the ingrown and embedded obstacles to popular participation: the men and interests threatened by a transfer of power.

Notwithstanding this resistance, the idea of decentralization is making its first timid and tentative appearances in political rhetoric. It is possible to predict that the first party to carry this banner (if buttressed by a solid program) will find itself on the right side of the decisive issue of the 1970's. At the moment the idea hovers elusively between liberal Democrats and liberal Republicans. Both face built-in political barriers. For the Democrats it is the difficulty of overcoming ideological attitudes which place the burden of salvation on Washington. For Republicans it is the more obstructive necessity to mollify those conservative elements which oppose any social action by government, whatever the techniques.

Yet the issues involved in decentralization are remote from the old struggles over states' rights and big government. Those struggles centered on the question of whether any effort at all should be made to solve social problems through collective action and public resources. Decentralization, however, assumes that this question is resolved affirmatively, and sees the issue is one of structure and organization (and power). Even modern conservatism is moving closer to a benign view of decentralization. In his campaign for mayor of New York, Mr. William Buckley argued for city action against problems ranging from air pollution to the scarcity of bicycle paths. He opposed federal intervention because it was "none of their business," making his objections to government action more geographical than ideological.

Although decentralization is designed to help combat the social and spiritual ills of fragmentation, it also responds to the fact that centralized bureaucracies tend to become increasingly ineffective and coercive in direct proportion to the scope and intricacy of the problem they are established to solve. This was less apparent when much of government action consisted of grants, subsidies, or insurance for individuals. It is not difficult to write checks. Now, however, we must apply complete technical and planning skills to wide-ranging difficulties. One need only look at the fantastic labyrinth of welfare programs, the monstrous incapacities of the Department of Health, Education and Welfare—operated by one of the best teams of executives in government—as well as the foreseeable futilities of the new Departments of Housing and Urban Development and Transportation, to realize that something is wrong with the old approach.

Decentralization would not only shift responsibility to state and local government. Private groups would also be involved, either by government (as in the community action program of the war against poverty) or through their own, self-generated efforts. By thus directly engaging individuals, and giving them a sense of participation and commitment, we could stimulate the desire for goals toward which many remain indifferent or even hostile while they are the province of a removed and abstract central government. If, for example, we could involve large numbers of Americans in programs of help to underdeveloped countries, they would become increasingly convinced, and even passionate, about the moral and political necessity for such programs.

Responsibility is the breeder of ability, and by assigning responsibility for important matters—decentralization would help improve the talent engaged in local government. Hours are spent in town councils arguing about the placement of new traffic lights, while the great issues are debated in Washington. It is little wonder that men of vitality and ability are reluctant to serve or else quickly lose their enthusiasm. Even so, the importance of political life is already attracting more able men into local public service, and the ability to solve problems is becoming a requirement of election to state houses and city halls.

Decentralization is not abdication. It is possible, as I will outline, to set standards for local action and by enforcing these standards to raise the level of performance. Different problems will call for different structures, requiring a great deal of political creativity and experiment. But there are common obstacles and methods of approach.

In a moment I will discuss some specific examples, but the guiding principle should be the transfer to local government or private groups of the needed resources, and the responsibility for decision, action, and policy in accordance with national standards of varying degrees of specificity. We are already doing this, to some extent, in programs ranging from the war against poverty to the construction of waste treatment plants on our rivers. (Standards, incidentally, can be educational rather than coercive. Often local groups are unaware of the dimensions of a problem, nor can they command the technical and intellectual resources necessary to devise solutions. A small but fascinating model of the educational approach is the President's Committee on Physical Fitness. That committee drew up model programs of physical training for schools, community organizations, and individuals. Though it had no regulatory power and hardly any money, the result has been a flourishing of physical-fitness programs across the country. The same technique might well be applied to the formulation of model school curricula, child-care centers, traffic-control programs, etc.)

The fact that local government lacks the resources—financial and human—to cope with even its present difficulties is a powerful barrier to decentralization. Walter Heller has proposed that the federal government simply turn over, presumably on a per capita basis, some of its revenue to the states. I am a great admirer of Mr. Heller and respect the liberal impulse behind his idea. It is, however, a counsel of defeat. It anticipates that Congress will react to rising revenues by cutting taxes rather than by helping the poor or rebuilding our cities, and it hopes to forestall this by transferring revenue out of congressional hands and out of the national budget (an objective which some conservatives have not fully understood). Thus the Heller Plan assumes that the politics of inertia—where programs are neither eliminated nor substantially increased—will dominate the federal structure. It also subsumes the praiseworthy faith that state governments will use this money for critical public needs. Actually, however, some will use it well and some will not. Depending on what the states do with the money, the Heller Plan may or may not increase the resources available for social problems, and could even lessen them. I expect that a higher level of local ability and public purpose will be set by the mounting responsibilities which come with decentralization. This does not mean, however, that the necessary ability and integrity are *already* sitting in every state house, crippled only by lack of money. It is a notorious fact that many state legislatures are more responsive to private interests, from loan companies to home builders, than is the Congress. Under the Heller Plan, it is quite possible that New York residents may end up paying federal taxes to reduce the tax burden on property owners in Indiana. Moreover, some assurance is needed that revenue collected across the nation is not sent to areas where its benefits are denied to Negroes.

Many of these problems can be avoided, and state competence raised, by turning resources over to the states for concrete purposes and with specific standards of performance, rather than by lump-sum payments. In addition, we may find that it is not the state but the city or smaller communities and private groups which are the appropriate units of action. Decentralization should go further and deeper than the state house. The Heller Plan might be worth trying if there were no alternatives, but there are many alternatives. They vary in the extent to which they restrict and direct state and local use of nationally collected resources. They provide a great deal more flexibility and a strengthened assurance that critical needs will be met. Since I am not an economist, I only speak in general terms about matters which are highly technical in detail.

First, we can establish federal standards and guidelines in specific areas—e.g., housing or pollution control—and allocate funds to the local units which meet the requirements. This is the structure of the anti-pollution program for rivers and the new Demonstration Cities Act.

Second, there is the possibility of credits against federal income taxes for additional state taxes that would be earmarked for particular purposes like education. There would have to be some safeguards against the transfer of state revenues to other purposes in order to reduce local taxes, and perhaps also a rising base line could be established which would take growing state population and wealth into consideration.

Third is a variant of the Heller Plan: general appropriations to local authorities for a variety of specified purposes, such as health, education, housing, training, etc., allowing the state or locality to set its own priorities. Of course, tax credits can be used in the same way.

I am sure there are other fiscal devices (for example, allowing states to require tolls on the interstate highway system if the revenues are devoted to certain public purposes) which might also serve to increase the resources available to states as an instrument of decentralization.

Money and programs are useless without competent people to administer them. Although imaginative political leadership will sometimes recruit men of unusual ability (as Richard Lee has proved in New Haven), human skill is harder to find than cash, both because able men are not often attracted to local government and because we lack trained people. As greater responsibility flows outward from Washington, and as the work of states and communities becomes more important, public life will become more and more attractive. We will, however, have to make a generous national effort to train people for public service—something we have been slipshod about even at the federal level, where the defect has become more serious as problems have become more technical.

Again the viable techniques are numerous. Let me mention a few possibilities: federal grants to universities to establish training programs, perhaps even a foundation similar to the National Science Foundation; federally financed training institutes, for young men or established civil servants, either under national auspices or under the control of regions or states; subsidies for the salaries and expenses of highly skilled people; model codes for government workers, embracing incentive, tenure, recognition, etc. Perhaps a Governors' Conference could set such projects in motion. Many similar things are already done in other fields. For example, federal effort—seed money as well as full support—has enormously increased the number and quality of men and women engaged in scientific research. Certainly public service is no less important. Of course, even this effort will not coerce able men into public service, although it may help multiply their numbers and develop their talents. However, the Peace Corps and poverty program, the civil rights movement, and my own observations across the country have convinced me that large numbers of our citizens are seeking some effective way to serve society, and they are often willing to give up the attractions of private life for such an opportunity. If we do not provide them with the chance, our most valuable national resource will be dissipated.

I do not wish to elaborate on the many concrete areas where decentralization of activity is immediately practical. These will be limited only by our political and technical inventiveness. We already have several experiments to point the way. Still, it would be unfair not to give a few specific examples of realistic applications. I will sketch these examples in general terms. Carrying them out will require rigorous and detailed work. The Peace Corps was a few sentences in a campaign speech. The law establishing it takes up many pages.

To begin with the most difficult area of all, foreign policy: it is desirable and possible, and it may even be necessary, to turn over a substantial part of the foreign assistance program to state administration. Let me give an example of what I mean. The single most important economic problem for the developing countries is agriculture. The large majority of their populations work the soil. Agricultural development is essential for food, to lessen dependence on foreign imports (thus conserving foreign exchange), and to provide a market for industry by raising the income of farmers. The United States has an enormously successful agricultural economy, and the skill, know-how, and energy which built that economy can be found in the states rather than Washington—in the great agricultural universities, state departments of agriculture, and among private associations of farmers and growers. Several years ago it was proposed to President Kennedy that we ask a particular state government to administer our agricultural development program in a specified country or countries, giving the state all federal money set aside for this purpose. He was enthusiastic and wrote two or three personal memoranda to the State Department urging action.

The subsequent inaction was a dramatically illuminating example of the ability of a bureaucracy to frustrate a president. Nevertheless, it could not ignore him entirely. The first project (which was to be "experimental" even though the President had already decided on the general policy) was to ask the state of California to run the agricultural program in Chile. California has many of the same problems and crops, similar variations in climate, and even looks like a very fat version of Chile. Its population is larger, with approximately the same acreage of arable land, and it still manages to export 80–90 per cent of its production while Chile has to import food. I was a member of the team which went to Sacramento to discuss the project with Governor Brown. He was as enthusiastic as the President had been, and nearly all the concerned officials of his government shared his enthusiasm. They devoted many hours to planning and discussion, promised to invest substantial energy in the program, and to hire additional people. All this culminated in the signing of an agreement in the White House by the President and the Governor.

The project has not lived up to expectations, primarily because AID was unwilling to let go of the responsibility for a large part of its program. Yet it is just this kind of delegation of full control with its political and dramatic impact which is essential to any statewide feeling of significant participation. The arguments for it are, in my view, overwhelming. The states are better at agriculture than AID can ever hope to be and would do a better job. Although the states would be spending federal money, the drama, the publicity, and the fact that leadership was coming from the state house would inevitably summon widespread contributions of money and talent from the private sector and local government. Growers' groups might offer technical assistance, while high schools might establish exchange programs. Communities would "adopt" counterpart communities in the developing country. The possibilities are endless, and enough of them began to appear in California to prove they were realistic.

Such a program would give thousands of individuals and organizations the chance to participate in one of the most important overseas ventures of the American nation. In the process we could help create a broader political constituency for foreign aid. No longer would foreign aid be a remote endeavor through which a few anonymous bureaucrats in Washington hand over large chunks of taxpayers' money to equally remote people in some unknown capital. There is little doubt of the basic compassion of Americans toward other countries or of their interest in the people of foreign lands. Any foreign visitor who has lived here for a while can testify to that. But the current program does not touch these basic emotions, because it is abstract and removed. As a result, the foreign-aid program, morally imperative and vital to our interest, is doomed. It was that sense of impending doom which helped explain President Kennedy's interest. And the intervening years have seen a steady erosion of a most generous and necessary concept until its relationship to the problem is ludicrous, pitiful, and tragic. The 1966 election is an ominous augury that we may even be facing its extinction.

Another prospect for decentralization, and one closer to home, is the American city. We know that the problem of the cities is enormously complex. It is not one problem but a hundred: urban renewal and rehabilitation of rundown structures, new financing techniques and private development corporations, control of land speculation and new suburban slums, breaking up ghettos and giving people a place to play in, efficient transportation and mastery of the automobile. We may need to rebuild entire central cities or construct huge new satellite metropolises. The condition and future prospect of our cities are the greatest single threat to the quality of American life. Many who live in major urban areas are already the victims of conditions which confine, stifle, and degrade their daily existence to an extent unthinkable half a century ago. Nor is this a problem for the poor alone. They are the chief victims, but all must breathe the air, fight the traffic, do without nature, and worry about violence.

Instead of a scattered attack on particular problems we must begin by asking what kind of city we want to live in, and what kind of city we want for our children. As we approach the problem on this spacious scale, we see immediately that uncontrolled growth and change must be replaced by long-range planning which encompasses the entire urban area across municipal and state lines. And we see, too, that the cities do not have the money to meet their problems.

I believe we should adopt a Marshall Plan approach to the problems of the American city. Resources on a large scale would be made available to those urban areas which prepared a comprehensive program for future development, embracing urban policies as diverse as land use, housing codes, tax structures, and water systems. The federal government could give technical assistance in planning, set certain standards, and ensure that the program was being carried forward. But the basic responsibility for decision and action would rest with the city and its people. This would not only help meet the more general imperatives of decentralization, but would provide a powerful incentive for the cooperation across historical political jurisdictions which is the condition of effective action.

There are many other areas in which decentralization is possible. Antipoverty and job-retraining programs should be increasingly handed over to community groups instead of being drawn, as they now are, closer to the federal government. Aid to education might well be administered to a far larger degree by local boards, subject only to the most general standards. Instead of threatening to draft all young Americans for public service, we could encourage and finance a host of varied volunteer groups to perform public services at the state and community level in order to provide an outlet for those many citizens still anxious to find an answer to the question, *What can you do for your country?* Many federal installations and services could well be subject to greater local supervision. For example, we might establish local boards of directors for post offices, permitting the community to decide, within the limits of available resources, the kind of postal service they require, even hire and fire postmasters and, at least, to air their complaints.

Much of this will appear sloppy and chaotic. Some of it will certainly be confused. It is always easier to yearn for the illusory neatness of central direction and control, under the assumption that it is more effective. That assumption has often proved wrong in the past, and it must now be questioned across the board of federal activity. Even if we do add to confusion, that is a small price to pay for the benefits of decentralization. Confusion may even turn out to be creative. In fact, I cannot remember a single unconfused government organization that ever produced an important new idea.

I do not assume that proposals such as these will cure what Norman Mailer calls "the plague" of modern life or halt the flow toward fragmentation and futility. Politics is only part of the story. The values, ideas, and instincts of our modern condition may be too relentless to yield, even slightly, to leadership and political invention. Perhaps the changes required are far more convulsive and profound than most of us can formulate. As a practicing politician, I can only hope for and speak of those things which seem to reach toward the limits of foreseeable possibility.